Welcome to the Stage

Welcome to the Stage

How A Forgotten Dream Became A Reality

ED REGINE

WELCOME TO THE STAGE
HOW A FORGOTTEN DREAM BECAME A REALITY

iUniverse books may be ordered through booksellers or by contacting:

iUniverse
1663 Liberty Drive
Bloomington, IN 47403
www.iuniverse.com
844-349-9409

ISBN: 978-1-6632-1039-5 (sc)
ISBN: 978-1-6632-1040-1 (e)

Print information available on the last page.

iUniverse rev. date: 10/30/2020

Contents

Introduction

I wrote this book mostly from memory using very few resources. My grandparents, my parents, all my aunts and uncles, and my five siblings are no longer with us. The only source of information was my recollections. I will take an oath, a lie detector test, I will look you in the eye and tell you that every word in this book is the truth to the best of my knowledge. I did not embellish; I did not exaggerate. I just wrote it from the contents stored in my memory banks. I hope in some small way this book will inspire anyone who has dreamed of doing something they loved but somehow that dream got lost along the way. I can assure you that dream is still out there. Go for it. You can make it happen. You will never know unless you try. I guarantee it is never too late.

Sincerely,
Ed Regine

Prologue

June 1993- I am sitting in the dressing room backstage at one of the most prestigious venues in America, The Greek Theater in Los Angeles, California. In a few short minutes, I am going to perform in front of approximately 6,000 people and as that thought entered my mind, I began to relive the extraordinary journey that got me here. Suddenly I heard the stage manager say, "Five minutes Mr. Regine". I refocused and put the finishing touches on myself and headed out of my dressing room. As I reached the wings (side of the stage) I became engulfed in so many emotions I could hardly compose myself. I peeked out at the crowd and the theater was filled to near capacity.

This was such an overwhelming situation, the most important show of my career. I thought, I've got to get this right.

Just then I heard the stage manager say, "One-minute Mr. Regine." My heart began to race, the adrenaline was pumping, suddenly this strange thought came over me that my waiting to go on stage was like Neil Armstrong sitting in that capsule waiting to blast off to the moon. The excitement, the fear, the anxiety, the doubt that he must have felt seemed so relatable to me. Then just at that moment I heard those amazing words that always soothe my soul and make all else disappear. Four simple words.

"Welcome to The Stage."

Chapter 1

My very first appearance was on a cold wintery night in 1946 as my mother was ready to deliver a much-anticipated Christmas gift. Waiting anxiously for me to arrive were my five siblings, the oldest was my sister Anne who was nineteen, next in line was my sister Joan, she was fourteen, then came my oldest brother, Joseph who was ten years old, next my youngest sister Antonia who was six and finally my older brother Francis who was four years old. My mom loved nicknames, so we all had them. Anne's nickname was "Queenie" because she was first and that made her a Queen. My sister Joan was nicknamed "Tootsie" because my mom said as a baby her arms and legs were like a tootsie roll. Next was Joseph and because he was the first boy my mom dubbed him "Sonny". My mom said my sister Antonia was a beautiful baby just like a doll, so she was nicknamed "Dolly". Finally, my brother Francis who my mom said was a big and strong baby, so he was nicknamed "Duke". Rest assured I would eventually get one. As a toddler I would hope around in my crib like a bunny rabbit thus my nickname was "Bunny". My mom give birth to me at home. My dad was there, my oldest sister Anne would help and, of course, there was Dr. DiSalvo who was there to deliver me. My mom labored throughout the night and into the next day. So, the special Christmas gift was going to be late. Early in the afternoon on December 26, 1946, my mom finally gave birth to a bouncing baby boy. The sixth and final installment to the Regine Family. My birth evened the score of 3 boys and 3 girls. Ironically, for reasons I never got to know, all three girls were born in the hospital and all three boys were born in the house. My mom and dad had agreed when they got married that my mom would name any female child and my dad would name all male children. So, my dad got to name me, and he did it in a peculiar way. He loved the actor Edward G. Robinson, so he went with Edward, the problem he had was Edward G. Robinson was only a stage name; his real name was Emanuel Goldberg. I do not think my dad knew that. Anyway, because Edward G. Robinson was his stage name the "G" did not stand for anything. So, my dad decided to take the "G" and use it to name me after his favorite cowboy, Gene Autry. So, I was named Edward Gene Regine. Obviously, my dad did not think this through. As soon as my mom delivered me, the doctor said, "We have a problem." This frightened my parents. My dad asked, "What's wrong?" Dr. DiSalvo said he wasn't sure what was wrong, but he did say he hadn't seen anything like this before and my dad should take my mom to the hospital in hopes that they would know what was going on. Being born and raised in Providence, Rhode Island, my dad took my mom, with me in her arms to the closest hospital, which was aptly named Rhode Island Hospital. My mom and I were taken into an examination room where, after a while, a team of doctors entered the room. The doctors had done an extensive examination and explained to my mom and dad as best they could what was going on. They told my parents that I had bladder and intestine issues and they said quite frankly they didn't have the full knowledge of what had happened, and they flat out told my parents they couldn't correct what was going on. My parents were devastated. But my mom refused to give up. She did some research and discovered there was a John Hopkins children's center in Maryland that was considered one of the world's greatest hospitals. My dad was the sole provider of our family, driving a taxi 12 hours a day, 6 days a week. My mom was dead set on taking me to John Hopkins to get the medical help I needed. Sadly, my dad could not afford to take time out of work, so my mom decided to go alone. She loaded me on a train because my mom did not drive, and we headed to Baltimore. With me bundled up her arms, she walked into John Hopkins and said, "I need someone to look at my baby." My mom was taken to a kind of consultation room where she told her story. After a short wait, a team of several doctors came in and asked my mom if they could take a look at her son. She agreed and my mom and I were taken to an examining room where I was giving a thorough exam. After the examination was over, we were taken back to the consulting room where the team of doctors began to explain what was going on. They told my mom I was born with what they called a ureter sigmoid. My mom said, "What does that mean?" One of the doctors said that my stomach walls were thin when I was born thus pushing my bladder through and I would need several surgeries to correct the problem. The doctor then went on to explain that John Hopkins could do the surgeries, but because we lived in Rhode Island it would be taxing on the family to have it done in Maryland. The doctors assured my mom that the Boston Hospital Children's Medical Center would be more than capable of taking care of my medical needs and John Hopkins would handle all the pertinent paperwork. My mom agreed and when we arrived home she explained to my dad what was going on. We had to make the appointment on my dad's day off so he could drive us to Boston and meet with the doctors. When we arrived, we were sent to an examination room. Shortly thereafter a doctor entered. His name was Dr. Hardy Hendren. Dr. Hendren explained the procedures that would be needed and assured us he would perform all the necessary operations. Dr. Hendren is still with us as I write this. He is 92 years old and has distinguished himself as a world-renowned surgeon and has amassed some of the highest awards in his field. My first surgery occurred when I was incredibly young. I do not recall any of it, but word was I had a hernia and Dr. Hendren thought it best to remove it while I was still an infant. After the surgery Dr. Hendren said the more extensive operations were to come, but he thought it best to wait and let me grow a little and then came back for the first major surgery. In the interim, my mom took great care of me as we waited for Dr. Hendren to give us the word. As I was approaching my third birthday, Dr. Hendren scheduled the first of 5 major surgeries. Obviously, I don't remember that operation, but it was more or less an exploratory operation of my plumbing and what the doctor would need to do moving forward. My mom wanted to stay in Boston for the surgery and my recovery, but Dr. Hendren explained that I would receive the best of care and that it would be too hard on my mom. Reluctantly, she agreed. The operation went well, and I was back home. The next surgery occurred when I was 5 years old. This operation was the beginning of the reconstruction process. Dr. Hendren did a masterful job and the operation was a complete success. I was halfway there. Due to my surgery and the healing process, I was unable to attend school. Fortunately, my oldest brother "Sonny" was extremely intelligent, and he would informally teach me many things. It was sort of his version of what we call today as being homeschooled. When I was finally cleared to attend school, I was 8 years old. I was put into first grade, but on the first day, I was immediately moved up to the 3rd grade, thanks to my brother Sonny. To give you an idea of his intelligence, he once beat the Rhode Island chess champion, and he did it while he was blindfolded. I was turning twelve years old and Dr. Hendren wanted to be finished with the final two surgeries before I entered puberty. I was scheduled to have one operation, go home for two weeks, and then return for the final surgery. But Dr. Hendren consulted with my parents and they unanimously agreed to have me stay to get them both done. I recall they were tough surgeries, but I came through it and it all went extremely well. One incident sticks out in my mind. When I was young, and even to this day, I have an exceedingly difficult time swallowing a pill. So, after numerous failed attempts to take my medication orally, the hospital asked if I could handle my medication if it was administered in needle form. I said okay because I never had a problem getting a shot. Well, I was so good at it that when I was to receive a shot, the nurses would take me into the younger patients' room and have them watch me get the needle. I never flinched thus showing the other kids it is not that bad at all.

Another incident I recall was, as I was recovering from one of my surgeries when I was eight years old, I noticed a large rectangular bandage on my stomach. I assumed that was where the surgery took place.

One day at the Children's Medical Center, a nurse's aide or candy striper as they were called back then, came into my room and said she was taking me to the courtyard to get some fresh air and some sunshine. She walked me down in my cart which was more like a soapbox than a piece of hospital apparatus. It was made of wood and had a backing so you would be in a sitting position and it was long enough to stretch your legs out. As I was sitting in the courtyard, I noticed two of Boston's finest came in on horseback. They dismounted and let some of the children pet their steeds. What happened next was exciting. The officers began putting kids in the saddle and walking them around the courtyard. I wanted in.

When they came around by me, I asked for a ride and they complied. It was awesome being on one of these amazing animals. Somehow, word got out as to what I did because when I got back to my room all hell had broken loose. The nurse on duty told me to get in bed. I no sooner got settled when a cadre of doctors entered my room. There were seven or eight of them who formed a semi-circle around my bed. One of the doctors was my surgeon Dr. Hendren. I could tell he seemed upset and concerned. He approached me, pulled back the bed sheet, and began removing the huge bandage. That was the first time I saw the incision and it still had the stitches in.

Luckily, all the stitches were intact and there were no signs of damage to the incision. Dr. Hendren did a quick examination of the area and seemed relieved that no damage was done.

He then told the nurse to put on a fresh bandage and left followed by the other doctors. The entire incident caused quite a stir and was the topic of conversation for several days that followed.

At this point, I want to give a special thank you to my parents, especially my mom who showed so much love for me that she fought on my behalf to get me the medical attention I needed and the special care she gave me through my ordeal. Without her dogged determination, who knows what would have happened to me. Also, a heartfelt thank you to Dr. Hardy Hendren, who did a masterful job throughout my surgical process.

Chapter 2

We lived in an almost exclusive Italian section of Providence called Federal Hill until I was almost five years old. I have no clue how, but somehow, my parents bought a three-decker house for $9900.00, so we left Federal Hill and moved to South Providence. One of the main reasons they bought that house was that my mom loved lilac bushes and the backyard of this house was loaded with them. The plan was to live on the second floor and use the other floors as rentals. When my parents bought the house, the third floor was already rented to the Burke family which consisted of a mom and her twenty-something son, Walter. They were incredibly quiet and respectful and paid their rent like clockwork. The first floor was empty at the time of purchase, so my dad did some paintwork, installed new linoleum and started renting it out. Things did not go well. People would rent out the first floor but after a couple of months, they would move out in the middle of the night sticking my dad for the rent. Although the Burkes stayed, the first floor became a revolving door. Also, the house was in poor repair, the boiler was weak and in the winter the pipes would freeze and burst and create all sorts of problems. The electrical system was not that great either. Even plugging in the toaster would sometimes result in blowing a fuse. After approximately seven years, the Burkes moved out, the repairs kept mounting and my dad was unable to rent out the first or third floor.

It came to a point where my dad could no longer maintain the property. I do not know if my dad sold it, auctioned it, or just gave it away.

All I remember is we were out of there. We moved into several different places over the next few years, until the early sixties when my oldest sister Anne bought a two-family house in Providence.

My parents and I moved into the first floor and Anne rented the second floor to my sister Antonia. That was the last time I had lived with my parents as I moved out after I got married in May of 1967.

I remember growing up we had a 17" black and white television with just a couple of channels. I recall as a young child I would sit on the brightly colored linoleum floor in our TV room with my mom and dad and a couple of my younger siblings watching TV shows like The Ted Mack Original Amateur Hour, the Honeymooners, The Ed Sullivan Show, Milton Berle, as well as Sid Caesar's Your Show of Shows. As I watched these shows, I would be become mesmerized. I was deeply fascinated by all the comedians and their ability to make people laugh. There was something about making people laugh and hearing their laughter that made me feel amazing. My heroes back then were all the comedians I would see on television: people like George Burns and Gracie Allen, Bob Hope, Groucho Marx, Abbott and Costello, Milton Berle, Lucille Ball, Jack Benny, Rip Taylor, Frank Gorshin, Phyllis Diller, and Guy Marks. I'm sure I have left out a few, and I apologize for that. I loved watching all of them and wanted to be just like them. This was my dream: I wanted to be on TV and make the whole world laugh. I did not like school and for me, based on my dislike for school and the fact that my family wouldn't have the money, I knew higher education was not in my future and I didn't care. I just loved comedy so much that I could not focus when it came to school. I remember lying in bed at night with my little transistor radio listening to a radio station in Pennsylvania that played comedy albums and I was so impressed I would tell my friends the comedians' routines and they would laugh, and I would get this rush. It was an amazing feeling. People ask me all the time what made me want to become a comedian. Simple answer: I just absolutely love to make people laugh.

Ironically, my dad, in his younger days, was in vaudeville. He was part of a comedy team called Regan and Valle.

My dad's partner was a little short Italian man named Archie Villa. When they teamed up they decided to use the stage name of Regan and Valle. Originally, my dad was the funny guy with Archie playing the straight man. However, booking agents back then had an unwritten rule that the straight man would be the taller one and the shorter one the funny guy. My dad was only 5'6" however; Archie was 5'4" so my dad became the straight man. Remember, this was in the late 1920s to the early '30s. The act, for its day, was funny. The concept was the older brother, (my dad), who had been in America for a while, after coming from Italy, would try to explain to his younger brother (Archie) the slogans, phrases, and general information needed to assimilate into America.

Once my mom and dad had more children and vaudeville was dying out, my dad had to get a "real" job. Because of the stock market crash, jobs were scarce. My dad's older brother, my Uncle Mario, was a taxi driver and when my dad was struggling to find work, Uncle Mario suggested my dad get a commercial driver's license which would enable him to drive a cab. My dad took his advice and drove a taxi for the next forty-plus years. After Archie left Vaudeville he become a thoroughbred horse trainer at a small racetrack in the rural town of Pascoag, Rhode Island. Because my dad and Archie were such good friends my dad would attend the races and check with Archie to see if he had any good tips. As a good friend, he would always give my dad inside information. Archie was extraordinarily successful and became the leading trainer at Pascoag for many years until a fire destroyed the track in April of 1948. In the meantime, a new track was being built in Lincoln, Rhode Island. It finally opened in 1947. It was built by B.A. Dario, who was the owner of the Pascoag Park Racetrack.

It was named Lincoln Downs. It was a smallish facility, with the grandstand accommodating approx. 6,000 spectators, plus 2,000 more in the diminutive clubhouse and turf club. The track was 13/16ths of a mile in circumference with relatively sharp turns, thus making it more favorable for front runners. (That fact will come into play later) Due to the fire, and thankfully none of Archie's horses were injured, he moved his stable over to Lincoln Downs. Whenever my dad got an opportunity he would go to the track. He really enjoyed the races. I recall after my surgeries; my dad would take my mom and me to the races. Mom and I would wait in the car close to the fence so I could see what was going on. My dad would come to the fence with hot dogs and soft drinks. I would watch the races through the fence, or what I could see of it, and it seemed so exciting to me. The more times I went, the more I became attracted to it.

The roaring of the crowd, the pounding of the hoofs, colorful jockeys, it was captivating to me.

When Lincoln Downs closed their racing season, most of the better stables would ship their horses to Suffolk Downs in Boston and Rockingham Park in Salem, New Hampshire.

The lesser stables would wait until summer to compete on the "Fair Circuit." The fair circuit consisted of a group of county fairs in Massachusetts that featured thoroughbred racing. There were county fairs in Brockton, Weymouth, Marshfield, North Hampton, and Great Barrington. My dad loved going to the fairs each year. I can remember as far back as 7 or 8 years old going the county fairs. The summer after my surgeries my dad took my mom and me to several of the county fairs. My mom would sit on the ground level and my dad loved to walk around. I liked going up in the grandstand to get a better vantage point to watch the races. On summer day at The Brockton Fair I was in the grandstand to watch the race. It was the middle of the card, either the 5th or 6th race, the horses were loaded in the starting gate, and a few seconds later the gates sprung open and they were off. You could hear loud cheering from the huge crowd as the race unfolded. The cheering reached a fever pitch as the field turned into the home stretch. Approximately 50 yards from the finish line, one of the lead horses tragically broke it's left front leg, causing a chain reaction spill. Three other horses had fallen, as well as their jockeys.

Fortunately, those three horses got to their feet and were uninjured. All four jockeys involved got up and suffered no serious injuries.

Sadly, the news for the horse that broke its left leg was not good. It was obvious that he had to be humanely destroyed. The crowd became eerily quiet. The trainer and groom of the horse tried to calm it down, but the horse was agitated, very factious, and extremely difficult to control.

Remember this, back in the late 50's, there were no lethal injections, no van to cart the horse off, not even a canvas to hide what was about to happen. And happen it did in plain sight. I apologize for being so graphic, but this is what I saw with my own eyes. A Massachusetts State Trooper removed his pistol from its holster, and he fired a shot into the horse's head. The crowd was horrified. I screamed at the top of my lungs, "Nooooooo!" What made this situation even more horrific was that the horse did not succumb to the gunshot. So, then the State Trooper fired a second round into the horse's head and that was the fatal one. I was bawling my eyes out, as were many of the fans in attendance.

What happened next was outright appalling. A tractor pulled up towing what I can best describe as a metal slab. Several horsemen worked together to roll the fallen runner onto the slab. Once that was completed, the tractor drove off and, mercifully, it was over. What I witnessed was one of the most gut-wrenching, heartbreaking experiences of my life. To this very day, that entire episode is burned in my memory and something I will never forget.

Chapter 3

In the summer on different occasions, before the fire at Pascoag, my dad would take me with him to Archie's stable to look at the horses. And I fell in love with these magnificent animals. So much so, that I thought doing what Archie is doing could be a great career for me and maybe someday I would become a famous horse trainer. This was the initial phase of losing sight of becoming a comedian. I still had the drive and determination, but because there was no opportunity in Rhode Island to become a comedian plus I didn't even know how to be a comedian. However, despite that, I continued to believe that one day it would happen. But being around horses was real, I could touch it, I could feel it, it was there for me to learn and become a famous horse trainer. Archie was extremely talented when it came to training a thoroughbred.

One day, while at the Pascoag track, Archie and my dad had a huge argument. What happened was when Archie would tell my dad that he believed his horse would win the race, my dad would tell all his friends and they would bet on Archie's horse. Those bets would lower the odds, and this made Archie so angry that he told my dad to never come to the stable ever again.

Because of that falling out, Archie and my dad never spoke to each other for the rest of their lives.

My dad was also a huge boxing fan. He was friends with a local guy named Leo P. Bradley. I don't know what the P. stood for, but Leo was a boxing promoter and manager.

Occasionally Leo and my dad would attend live boxing matches in our area. I recall once or twice my dad taking me and I found it to be overly exciting.

So, at a young age I became a boxing fan. My dad idolized Rocky Marciano and would argue with his friends and co-workers that Rocky was the greatest fighter of all time. He would have heated arguments defending Rocky as some of his friends thought that Joe Louis or Sugar Ray Robinson was the greatest. I can remember even at an incredibly young age how my dad would rave about Rocky and how Marciano beat Jersey Joe Walcott for the heavyweight title with a 13th round knockout of Walcott with a right-hand punch that to this day boxing historians consider the hardest punch of all time. The fight occurred on September 23, 1952, several months before my 6th birthday, but I still have a clear impression of it today. Nine months later the two fighters were scheduled for a re-match in Chicago on May 15th, 1953. I was now six years old, but I remember vividly how excited my dad was, looking forward to another great fight. So, on that night my dad was ready. He took the night off to watch it and that afternoon he went to the local Italian deli and bought salami, cheese, capicola, olives, bread and covered our linoleum floor with newspapers as he anticipated a great evening of boxing. The fight was broadcasted on network television as the Gillette Cavalcade of Sports.

My dad was pumped as he carefully adjusted the rabbit ears and settled in. Unfortunately, the night did not go as planned. Oh, Rocky won the fight alright by a knockout in the first round; however, it was fairly obvious from the opening bell that Jersey Joe did not want any part of this re-match. It appeared that after that first grueling fight, Walcott was only there for a payday. I think most boxing authorities would agree. My Dad was outraged. For many years as I was growing up my Dad would tell this story to anyone who would listen.

I had just graduated from Junior High School, and in September 1962, I would start high school. Most of my classmates went on to Central High School, a short walk from my house, but my guidance counselor suggested, against my will, that I attend Hope High School. This was on the other side of town, which required me to take two busses to get there. Although most, if not all my friends went to Central, I made some new friends at Hope. Because my mom did not drive and my dad needed to sleep late due to his job, taking the two busses were getting old quick, plus I couldn't stop thinking about how badly I wanted to be close to the horses. I thought about it constantly and finally reached a decision.

I planned to finish 10B (that was the grading system back then) and then sit my parents down and tell them I wanted to quit school and go to work at the racetrack. When I sat them down and told them, my mom just about had a heart attack. Not so much that I wanted to quit school, which was bad enough, but where I wanted to work. She was sure I would be around low life gamblers, hustlers, seedy-people and it was no place for a sixteen-year-old.

My dad, who generally ruled with an iron fist, was a little more rational. I think because he loved the track so much it softened his stance on the matter. However, he made it crystal clear that I would have to pay $15 a week (he called it Room and Board) and take care of my expenses like saving for a car, have money for gas, etc. The $15 covered a place to sleep and meals. He told me to think hard about it and I will discuss it with your mother. In reality, my dad would do whatever my mom wanted, but he did put up a good front.

After several days of meetings and consultations, which meant my dad was just waiting for my mom's decision, my parents agreed. She was reluctant but finally gave in. When I was 15 I had some small after school jobs. I worked at a little coffee shop as a busboy and I remember the owner Tony, telling me his brother Dominic had a shoeshine parlor in downtown Providence. So, I asked him if he would talk to his brother about letting me work on the weekends. Dominic agreed but for no pay just tips. I accepted the offer. For the next several months, I shined shoes on weekends and worked at the coffee shop to save money for a car. On December 26, 1962, I turned sixteen years old and quit high school. I went to Driver's Ed to apply for my driver's permit. I passed the test and was ready for my road test. My oldest brother, "Sonny", had let me drive my dad's car, a 1953 Plymouth, (a standard shift) a few times and I had a couple of older friends who also gave me a turn at the wheel. I took my road test on a stick shift and passed with a score of 97%. I lost 3% for not turning my wheels to the curb on a hill.

When I left the shoeshine parlor and coffee shop I had saved some money, hopefully enough to buy a car. Oh yes, my dad did agree to register the car under his name, which gave him the authority to take it away from me if I didn't follow the rules. My driver's license was sent to me in early January 1963. Now it's all about finding a car. My dad agreed to take me car shopping, which consisted of my dad finding ads in the newspaper under the heading of "automobiles for sale."

My first car and this may sound hard to believe, was a 1953 Chevy Bel Air convertible, powder blue with a dark blue convertible top. Are you ready for this? I purchased this car for $35.00. Now, it needed a lot of cosmetic work, but it ran great and it was a standard shift and the clutch worked fine. I still had money left over for the registration fees, which was less than $20, and a couple of weeks of board money.

A couple of days before Lincoln Downs opened its winter racing season in February of 1963, I went there looking for a job. I read where most of the racing stables had already arrived, so this would be a good time. I walked from barn to barn asking the trainers if they needed help. Finally, after a half dozen or so attempts, I came upon a barn where a young man and an older gentleman were standing there. I just assumed the older man must be the trainer. I told them I was looking for work.

Just then, the young man walked over and asked if I had ever walked race horses before. He was the trainer and his name was Gary Hemmerling. After telling him my experiences at Archie's barn, he hired me. $35 a week and a $5 bonus if any of the horses in the stable win a race. He told me to be there at 6:00 am the next day. I was jubilant. I was so excited I could hardly wait to tell everyone.

Gary had a string of approximately 8-10 head in his barn and also a pony. Full-grown horses that are part of a stable but are not thoroughbreds are called Ponies. Our pony was a huge Appaloosa, beautifully dappled in white and brown, and his name was "Moose". Gary would use Moose to pony his runners in the morning, which means Gary would ride Moose while holding a racehorse and they would jog around the track as part of their training regimen. Occasionally, I would get to ride Moose and it was incredibly special. He was kind and gentle and I loved him. He was a great animal. Gary also had a German Shepard named "Killer" who was an awesome dog and I loved being around him. It was a friendly environment and I was incredibly happy working there. I became close friends with our groom, Willie. Notice him in the pictures at the back of the book. He was a cool guy who lived on the racetrack. He had his living quarters in the tack room, a place where the equipment would be stored. Bridles and saddles mostly. It felt like a family. However, Gary Hemmerling was not one of the sharpest trainers out there. Only one horse from Gary's original stable, Professor Sam, (check the photo at the end of the book) won a race in sixty days. The other three races we won were from horses Gary claimed from other trainers. Claimed means by entering your horse in a claiming race you are willing to allow your horse to be claimed from you by another trainer for the specified claiming price of the race. One horse in particular Gary claimed was a beautiful horse named Earl of Tyrone.

Gary claimed him from a trainer named John Mazza. Earl of Tyrone was John's only horse. When Gary claimed him, John was heartbroken. I would see John in the morning in the track kitchen, a place where grooms and exercise boys and the hot walkers would gather to have coffee, etc. He would ask how Earl was doing. I told him he is doing fine. John told me he thought Gary did the wrong thing by claiming his only horse.

Thirty minutes before the race that Earl of Tyrone won, (check the photo at the end of the book) Gary knew that John had put a claim in for him. As noted, Earl of Tyrone won his race and after the race, I took Earl to the spit box, a place where horses are taken for a saliva and urine sample. When I arrived, John Mazza was there himself to pick him up. It was sad to see "Earl" go as I fell in love with him. He was a magnificent thoroughbred. I also felt happy that "Earl" got reunited with John.

The meet was ending and Gary, who was from Ohio, had made plans to ship his horses to Detroit Racecourse in Michigan. When I told this to my mom, she nearly fainted. She objected feverishly and emotionally, forbidding me from going. I was upset, sad, and emotional, but in the end, I agreed not to go. As for Lincoln Downs, it closed for thoroughbred racing in 1976 and reopened in 1977 as Lincoln Greyhound Park. In July of 1991 It began simulcasting horse races from other tracks around the country.

In 2007 the old Lincoln Downs where I got my first job in horse racing was now known as "Twin River Casino".

Chapter 4

While all this was going on, my oldest brother "Sonny", who had rheumatic fever as a child which caused serious damage to his heart, was getting sicker. Finally, after a few severe episodes of suffering from shortness of breath resulting in family members administering mouth to mouth resuscitation, my parents took my brother to the hospital. The doctors told my parents and my brother his heart was so badly damaged that they gave him only one year to live. They went on to say, "We can perform a valve replacement procedure with a 50/50 chance of survival". When they came home my mom was hysterical, crying unashamedly my dad was consoling my mom and my brother was stoic. What a horrible option. Die in a year or possibly die on the operating table. My mom was vehemently against the surgery. My dad thought it would be worth the chance. Ultimately the final decision was my brother's. In true fashion, being the hero, he was, he opted for the surgery. I remember him saying "what choice do I have?" My brother "Sonny" survived the operation and lived for two weeks until his body rejected the artificial valve. The cause of death was pneumonia. The very last time I saw "Sonny" alive was at the hospital. He was sitting up and in a good mood. One of the foods he loved was snail salad. He asked my mom to bring him some My mom did, and he really enjoyed eating it. I was very hopeful he was going to be okay but the very next night we got a call from the hospital saying, "your son has turned for the worse." My mom and dad jumped in the car and rushed to the hospital. We all waited until they returned. When they came into the house, they did not have to say a word. We all knew "Sonny" had passed away. It was April 25th, 1963. He was 26 years old. To this day, I still think of him and how much he meant to me.

The loss of my brother Sonny had a profound effect on our family, especially my mother who mourned my brother's death until the day she died. My mother wore black clothing to mourn my brother's death for over forty years. The loss of my brother induced a fear in me to the point where I would feel like I would get a heart attack if I were active, so I would avoid any kind of sports or physical activity. It was so bad; my mom had me checked by a doctor who diagnosed me as having anxiety caused by my brother's death. The doctor prescribed Valium, which I took for a while, but then I stopped taking it and managed to get over my anxiety on my own.

So now, I am sixteen years old, the race meeting was over, my boss shipped out to Michigan, I lost my mentor, my hero, my big brother. So, things were not going so well for me. The racing season moved to Suffolk Downs in East Boston, Massachusetts. Commuting from Providence to Boston every day would be too much because of the condition of my car, so the only option was to live on the track.

But I wanted to stay around to help my mom who was not doing well due to the loss of my brother, and that's putting it mildly. From the time of my brother's death, until the day my mom passed she was never the same person I once knew.

After the Suffolk Downs meet would close, the horsemen would move to Salem, New Hampshire, to race at Rockingham Park. An even further commute so again I was faced with the same dilemma. The only option I could see was to stay home because I was not comfortable leaving my mom alone, especially at night. By this time, all of my older siblings had left the nest. So, with my dad still working the 4 pm to 2 am shift, I was the only one still living at home and the only one to spend the evenings with my mother. Now that I knew I would not be working at the track until the fall when Narragansett Park would open, I had to find jobs elsewhere. I had several different jobs that summer, including working at a Big Boy's, as a carpenter's helper and working for a house painter.

When the fall rolled around and Narragansett Park opened, I went back to work. Narragansett Park, which was affectionately known as "Gansett" opened on August 1, 1934. It was in Pawtucket, Rhode Island. In its heyday, no pun intended, "Gansett" was one of the premier racetracks in America with some of the biggest stables racing there, including Calumet

Farms, the Vanderbilt racing stable, and the Whitney stable. Some of the greatest horses in history raced at "Gansett" as well. Seabiscuit, War Admiral, Whirlaway, to name a few. The Great Seabiscuit actually won his very first race in 1935 at Narragansett Park. In 1942 Narragansett hosted a match race between 1941 Triple Crown winner, Whirlaway, and 1942 Preakness winner, Alsab, which drew an enormous crowd of 35,000 racing fans. The race was a thrilling spectacle and as the two great thoroughbreds hit the finish almost simultaneously It was Alsab who had won by a scant nose. The match race is considered by racing historians as one of the greatest races in thoroughbred history.

I hustled around the barns for several days doing freelance walking and stable work until I could find a trainer who would hire me on a permanent basis. Finally, I landed a steady job with a trainer named Ralph Browning.

I noticed how meticulous his operation was. Shed row, tack room, and his horses all looked amazing. He had a small stable of five head, which made me the only hot walker he needed. My first day with Ralph I spotted a horse in his stall with a huge blaze face. A blaze face is a horse with a wide swath of white on the front of its face. He looked familiar to me. I asked Ralph who it was, and he said it was a horse named Mecca Rose. I knew I recognized it. Mecca Rose was a big strong looking horse and as I recall he was trained by a guy named Bob Hansen; whose stalls were in our barn when I was working for Gary Hemmerling at Lincoln Downs. I remember seeing Mecca Rose every day, and although this big strapping horse looked the part, he seemed sluggish, docile and somewhat lazy. I told Ralph how I knew it was Mecca Rose and Ralph told me he claimed him at the end of the Lincoln Downs meet, and had been working on him all summer getting him ready for his first race as his trainer.

Ralph then told me to take Mecca Rose and walk him around the barn for thirty minutes. What he told me next surprised me. He said to put the shank in his mouth because he is a little hard to handle. A shank is a long leather strap with a chain attached to it. There is a clip at the end of the chain. The shank is clipped to a horse's halter for walking or jogging with a pony. So, I followed Ralphs's orders and put the shank through Mecca Rose's mouth and took him out of his stall. Folks, he nearly ripped my arm from its socket. This was not the docile animal I would see at Lincoln Downs. This was a powerful, massive racehorse. Ralph entered

Mecca Rose in a claiming race, and he won easily. No one claimed him so Ralph entered him next in an allowance race, a non-claiming race, and Mecca Rose won again. As the meet was ending, Mecca Rose had won seven races in a row until; finally, Ralph put him in a race with the best horses on the grounds and Mecca Rose's string of wins came to an end as he finished 4th. After that race, Ralph sent him to a farm for freshening after a grueling campaign.

Mecca Rose was a horse who epitomized what a thoroughbred is all about – speed, stamina, determination, grace, beauty, style, and courage. I will never forget Mecca Rose and if you attend horse racing make no mistake trainers know exactly what their horse is capable of. Ralph Browning proved to me that a different training regimen can make a world of difference and the results were obvious. Unfortunately, the racing fans who attend are not privy to this information. After many great years, Narragansett Park closed on June 29, 1979, and was sold to the City of Pawtucket Rhode Island. On May 30, 1981, the clubhouse was destroyed in a suspicious fire and it was never restored. The grandstand, believe it or not, became a huge flea market and later a rail-road salvage store.

I absolutely loved working around horses. My daily regime of working at the track consisted of me getting up at 5:30 in the morning, driving to the track, which was approximately seven miles from my house, working until 10:00 or 10:30, going home for an hour or so, then back to work in the afternoon. Some of my duties consisted of walking some of the horses around the barn for 30-45 minutes, filling their water pails, raking the shed row, cleaning the tack, and after a workout by one of our horses, assist in bathing them, and holding a horse while being attended to by a blacksmith.

In the afternoon, back to work refilling water pails, helping with the afternoon feed, and if we had a horse racing that day, I would cool it out after the race, which means walking while monitoring their water intake for approximately one hour. Narragansett would run until the end of November, and then there would be no racing in New England at all until Lincoln Downs opened in late February. A funny thing happened while working at Lincoln Downs. I recall I awoke one morning for work, and realized it was Friday, which was payday. I also realized I had hardly any gas in my car and only one thin dime to my name. Even though the racetrack was only seven miles away, I was sure I would not have enough gas to make it. However, I knew there was a Merit gas station less than a mile from my house. I also remember noticing that gas was 19.9 cents per gallon. So, I started doing the math. At 20 miles to the gallon, 10 cents would buy me a half gallon, so I could travel 10 miles. It was only seven miles to the barn so I knew could make it.

I drove to the Merit and pumped in 10 cents worth of gas. I made it to work with 3 miles to spare. That was the first and I'm sure the last time I would ever buy a gallon of gas for less than twenty cents. Times have certainly changed.

Chapter 5

I lost my virginity in a very unusual way. I was 16 years old working at the racetrack. Sometimes, after finishing my chores at the stable, I would sneak into the betting area. I didn't belong there as you had to be 18 years old, but it would be late in the day with perhaps one or two races left on the card and security would be scarce. On several occasions I'd wander into the clubhouse and I often noticed an older lady who was boisterous and would cheer loudly during a race. She was extremely attractive and had big blue eyes and blonde hair and a great figure. One day I said "Hi" to her, and we started a conversation. I told her I worked at the track and she told me how much she loved the horses and the races and to let her know of any hot tips. I told her I would and that someday I was going to be a great horse trainer. Our meetings and conversations went on for a couple of weeks. One afternoon in particular, she asked me how old I was, I told her I was sixteen. What she said next threw me for a loop. She asked me if I would like to go with her and get something to eat and what kind of food I liked. I told her I loved Chinese food. She told me that would be fine, and we should go in her car. I agreed. I recall her car was a stick shift. She said that she loved driving a standard shift and asked if I knew how to drive one.

I said "yes". Shortly thereafter, we got to the restaurant in downtown Providence; it was a typical Chinese restaurant with all the Asian accouterments. We continued talking during the meal and when we finished, we went back to her car. That is when things headed in an entirely different direction. She asked me if I ever went parking, which meant a lover's lane. Well, even though I was still a virgin I had many make-out sessions at the beach, at the drive-in, and in the car parking.

So, I told her I have, and she asked where I would go. I told her I knew a secluded road in Johnston, Rhode Island that is hardly ever used. She said "great". I directed her and approximately twenty minutes later we had arrived. It was pitch dark and somewhere around 7:30 pm. We chatted for a moment and suddenly we were making out. I must admit, I recall being very aroused. After several minutes of kissing, she dropped a bombshell; she asked me if I would like intercourse or oral sex. I was throbbing with excitement, but I knew I would feel uncomfortable exposing myself for oral sex, remember I was only 16 years old and lacked experience. I told her I would prefer intercourse. Things started happening fast. Clothing was being lifted or removed, positioning was very awkward, and once the logistics were worked out it was over very rapidly. We quickly put ourselves back together and headed back to the track to pick up my car. We talked on the way back, which consisted of your basic small talk. For the record, she was forty-one years old, but I will refrain from mentioning her name concerning any family members who may read this. After that night was over, I would see her from time to time at the races and we would talk, but the events of that night were kept silent. That was the only time that type of meeting ever occurred. I know by today's standards this would be a huge issue, and I certainly don't condone this behavior in any way shape or form. But back in the early '60s this kind of event would more than likely go unnoticed. I want to be clear; I was not molested; I wasn't forced into anything. It was something that I wanted and was a willing participant. Remember at 16 years old, my testosterone was raging. So, the entire episode had my head swirling with emotion. So much so that it blurred my reasoning of right from wrong. But times have certainly changed and by today's standards, this would have been sex with a minor, punishable by law, and I unequivocally agree!

I remember one morning which was like any other morning.

I woke up at 5 am, got myself ready, and headed off to work in my latest vehicle a 1955 Plymouth Belvedere Standard shift. By the opening of the "Gansett" meet, my Chevy Bel-Air had died. My dad took me to his mechanic, a guy named Joe who also sold a few cars on the side. He showed my dad this 1955 green Plymouth and told my Dad it ran great. It did not look like much, a lot of body rot, but I needed cheap dependable transportation, so we decided to take it for a test drive, and it ran super. My dad and Joe haggled for a while and we finally bought the car for $45.00. I digress. It was the morning of November 22, 1963, and I arrived at work at around 6 am. It was a busy morning and it went by quickly.

I finished around 10:30 am and because we had two horses entered that afternoon, I decided to stick around instead of driving home for a short stay and driving back to the track. I went to the track kitchen, had a bite to eat, hung around for a while, and then went back to the barn. By now it was noon and we had a horse in the first race. Post time for the race was 1 pm. So, the groom and I left the barn around 12:15 as we had to be in the paddock (the saddling area) 30 minutes before post time.

Our horse named Double Disc was the favorite in the race, but eventually finished fourth and the groom and I took Double Disc back to the barn. It was my job to cool him out, meaning walk him around for an hour while monitoring his water intake. As I was tending to Double Disc, an announcement came over the public address system. The President of the United States has been shot and the remainder of the program has been canceled. We were stunned. I had to finish my chores before I could leave. Once I was done with Double Disc, I immediately rushed home.

When I arrived, my mom was watching the news and she was crying. Walter Cronkite had just declared on national television that the President of the United States was dead. It was shocking, and for the next several days my family and I were glued to the television. The entire nation had come to a standstill except for the NFL which decided to play their games that weekend which, to me, was extremely disrespectful. I remember watching live, the flag-draped casket of the President as it made its way through Washington. I remember the First Lady dressed in black. I vividly remember little "John-John", JFK Jr., saluting his dad's casket as it went by. I felt so sad and lost. I recall watching live, Lee Harvey Oswald being escorted from a holding cell by law officers to a waiting van when Jack Ruby rushed in and shot and killed him. I saw this all with my own eyes on live television. It was so surreal and mind-boggling. People are asked all the time; do you remember where you were when President Kennedy was shot? My answer is yes, I remember crystal clear where I was. I was in the stable area of Narragansett Park in Pawtucket Rhode Island walking a thoroughbred racehorse name Double Disc.

Chapter 6

My parents had a stormy marriage, but they loved each other and stayed married for 58 years until my dad passed away. My mom was a farm girl from, at the time, rural Johnston, Rhode Island, an area filled with fields of vegetables. My dad was a "city slicker", born and raised in Federal Hill. My parents could not have been more opposite. They met at, a place called "The Hippodrome", a facility with an oval track where they presented bicycle racing. My uncle, Danny Piscione, was a prominent and successful bicycle racer, so my mom and a couple of my aunts would go to cheer their brother on. Because of my uncle, my mom and aunts were well known as the "Piscione Girls" my mom's maiden name. My dad, who enjoyed going to the bicycle races, heard about the Piscione Girls and wanted to meet them.

My dad had an impish sense of humor, so one night he purposely sat behind my mom and my two aunts to try to meet them. He "accidentally" dropped his pencil and asked the girls if they could pick it up for him. One of my aunts, Aunt Rose, was a country girl and ignored my dad completely. My other aunt, Sue, in so many words told him to get lost. However, my mom thought he was kind of cute and funny, so she handed him his pencil. To the dismay of my aunts, they started a conversation. At some point, my dad said to my mom, "if I can make you laugh could I have a date with you"? He proceeded with a volley of corny jokes and had my mom in stitches. The one thing my mom loved about my dad was he could make her laugh. It was my dad's goofy sense of humor that won her over.

The big hurdle now was to get the approval of my mom's parents, my grandparents. All four of my grandparents came from Italy, so winning them over was no small task. The night of the big date approval came, and my dad showed up in a fancy car he had borrowed from a friend. He was dressed in a suit and soft hat. His appearance did not sit well with my grandpa. He called him a "Federal Hiller," a bum, and not a hard-working farmer. Aunt Sue and Aunt Rose chimed in as well. Undaunted, my dad forged on with silly jokes, dopey stories and after a while, slowly but surely had convinced my grandparents that he was sincere, and they agreed to allow my mom to go on the date. At the time, my dad was 20 years old and my mom was 19 years old.

Approximately one year later, my mom and dad were married in late January of 1926. My mom moved away from the farm and they got an apartment in Federal Hill, where I was born. The address was 197 Cedar Street. As noted, it was an almost exclusive Italian neighborhood, with Italian markets selling Italian cheeses and cold cuts as well as many bakeries selling some of the Italian favorites like homemade cannoli, tiramisu, and more. At that time there still were pushcarts selling fruits and vegetables. Until he started performing in vaudeville, I recall my dad was involved in peddling fruits and vegetables. Or, as he would tell everyone, he was in the produce business.

After my parents were married, they would attend most of my Uncle Danny's races. One day, in particular, he was training to get ready for a big race against the reigning champion, who was known as Push 'Em Up Madonna. As he was finishing his training session, my uncle's coach called him to come in off the track. My uncle Danny said, "One more lap". While completing that final lap he took a spill and a large splinter from the wooden track stuck into my uncle's abdomen. This accident occurred in late 1928. Today he would have been fine, but back then they didn't have the drugs needed to combat the infection. The wound got infected and peritonitis set in. Sadly, at the age of twenty-eight my uncle passed away from that injury.

One year after their marriage, my parents had their first child, my oldest sister, Anne. She was born in late January 1927. Another girl came in 1930, my sister, Joan. Finally, a boy, my oldest brother, Joseph Jr. In 1936. Oops, another girl my youngest sister Antonia, in 1940. Another boy, my youngest brother Francis in 1942, and finally, yours truly in 1946. I had no idea at the time but by today's standards, we were most likely a dysfunctional family. None of us has any formal education. Not one of us graduated from high school.

My oldest sister Anne (Queenie) got a job as a waitress, and through hard work, living frugally, and never marrying, she did extremely well for herself by investing her hard-earned money in real estate. My sister Joan (Tootsie) never really held down a job and got involved with a married man and had a baby with him. Years later, she married and started living a normal life. My oldest brother (Sonny)was unable to work due to his heart condition and lived on some medical assistance from the state until his death.

I would just like to add, (Sonny) was an extremely intelligent person. I have never met anyone in my life with his uncanny talent to command such a wealth of knowledge.

He taught me so many things that I recall to this day. I admired him, I looked up to him, and loved him. He was my Hero. I often think of what he could have accomplished if he had good health.

My youngest sister Antonia, (Dolly) who at the age of sixteen, got involved with an older guy in his twenties. She got pregnant and they were scheduled to get married, but the night of the rehearsal dinner, he walked out and was never seen again. We had a naval base in Quonset Point Rhode Island and five years after my sister (Dolly) gave birth to my nephew, she met a sailor named Bobby Ray Brooks who was stationed at Quonset Point. He was from Arkansas, and after a brief romance he left the navy, and they were married. They moved to Johnston, Rhode Island, and together had five more boys. He became a lieutenant in the Johnston Police Department. When he retired from the force, they moved to Little Rock, Arkansas and my sister lived there with her husband and my nephews until her death.

Now comes my older brother, "Duke". He had incredible talent as an athlete, both in baseball and basketball. He was the tallest of the bunch at 6'1" which he inherited from my paternal grandfather who was well over six feet. As good as he was in sports; he did not give a damn about pursuing it. He despised school and would rarely attend. He also was not all that thrilled with work either. His passion was hustling card games and crap games. As young as 14 or 15 he would sponsor gambling with the local kids in our cellar. He followed the path of gambling the rest of his life.

After my 17th birthday, I waited until Lincoln Downs would open in early February to get back to work. As the meet opened, I noticed my brother, Duke, has gotten in with some guys who were at the racetrack betting on "The Call". It was a way to bet on a horse after the race had started. In the early sixties, many tracks had an "Open Bell" which meant once the race had started, anywhere from 6 to 12 seconds later a bell would ring which signified the betting windows were closed. What these guys would do is have someone with binoculars watching the starting gate. When a horse would jump out first he would use a hand signal to relay the number of that horse that was leading the race to a partner at the betting window who would receive the signal and call that number into the clerk. It was absolutely, positively legal. As I was working in the stables, I knew my brother was doing this, but I did not think much of it, until one day my brother pulled up in a brand new 1963 Chevy Impala, which he bought for $2,000 cash.

Now, this style of play was not a guarantee, but it did give an edge and create an opportunity to bet on a long shot you normally wouldn't, and on occasion a horse with long odds would break out first and go all the way to win, resulting in a huge financial return. As I watched my brother and others do this, it became fascinating to me.

I was still getting up in the morning and would jump from stable to stable as a freelance "hot walker," working for various trainers. Guys like George Handy, Norman Cardarelli, Johnny Ruth, and Frank Retzel, to name a few. Toward the end of the day, I would sneak into the betting area to watch my brother play the call. He was good to me at the time. If he had a good day, he would throw me a $10 or $20. When Lincoln Downs closed for their season, it also closed the chapter in my life of working on the race track. My brother and a guy nicknamed T. G. (because one day at the races he won Ten Grand) would go to Boston and New Hampshire to play the Call. Not always but almost all the time, and thanks to my mom coaxing him because she still believed the racetrack was not the ideal career for me, although strangely she thought life as a gambler was okay, my brother would take me along. He was not overjoyed about having me tag along, but he obeyed my mom's wishes. This went on until I reached the age of 18.

Chapter 7

In December,1964 I turned 18. My brother's partner, T.G., decided to move to Detroit after the holidays to play a racetrack in Michigan called (DRC) Detroit Race Course. This created an opening for me. One night while having dinner at my brother's house, he made me an offer to be his "take off" man starting in February of 1965 at Lincoln Downs winter meet. The deal was for 25% of the action. Let me explain, I would be stationed at the $50 betting window and would receive a hand signal from him, call it in the mutual clerk, who would punch out a predetermined amount of tickets, and then I would pay for them. I would also handle the betting money, cash all winning tickets, and most importantly, make sure I get the hand signals right.

My brother would bankroll the operation (meaning he would put up the money) and if we were in the red, I would have to make up the loss before I would gain any profit. That year, we played all four New England racetracks, Lincoln Downs, Suffolk Downs, Rockingham Park, and Narragansett Park. It was a profitable year and I started accumulating money and had a few thousand dollars stashed away. After the races were over for the day, at night I would meet up with several friends, and we would go dancing in clubs that featured, girls in sexy costumes dancing in cages. They were known as "Go-Go" dancers.

I was riding a gravy train, which I thought would never end. I had a cool car, a 1964 Chevy Impala Super Sport convertible, money stashed away, meeting girls in the clubs, oh yeah, the reason we could get in those clubs was the fact that we all had phony ID's. At the time there were such thing as a Photo ID, so it was a piece of cake getting in. As time went on, my brother kept increasing my cut until it reached 40% and he said that would be how it would stay. I was okay with it. We kept showing a profit and I kept putting money away.

What I am about to tell you is amazing and something Hollywood writers couldn't imagine. However, I swear it is unequivocally true. While playing the "call" at Lincoln Downs, the track introduced a new betting format called the "Twin Double". It worked this way. Bettors would wager on the 5th and 6th races. If successful in picking the winners of those two races the bettor would exchange that winning ticket for selections on the 8th and 9th races. If successful again, that bettor would have hit the "Twin Double" Occasionally a longshot would win one of those races, resulting in a huge payoff. My brother and I noticed there was a crew that came in from New York that would try to buy "live" tickets from bettors, meaning if a gambler had successfully picked the first two winners, the New York crew would offer to buy the ticket for the price of the parlay. The parlay would be the entire payoff of the 5th race winner bet on the 6th race winner. For example, if the winner of the 5th race paid out $10.00, that $10.00 would be bet on the 6th race winner, if that winner paid $20.00 the parlay would be worth $100.00. So aside from playing the "call", Duke and I would sometimes try to buy a ticket from a fan who had the first half winners just to take a chance on hitting the Twin Double. Remember, my dad always liked to go to the races on his day off and at times my mom would go with him. One day in particular my mom and dad were at the races. On this one unique day my brother and I were trying to buy a ticket from the first half of the "Twin Double", but it wasn't going to be easy because the winning horses of the first half (the 5th and 6th races) were extreme long shots. the parlay was approximately $800. Duke and I hung around the "Twin Double" exchange window looking for anyone with a "live" ticket. The New York Crew was there as well. I recall there was only one guy in our area who had a winning ticket and he absolutely would not sell. He swore he was going to win the "Twin Double". Just when it seemed hopeless who should approach us but my mom and dad. My dad generally played favorites (the most logical horses in a race), but my mom was what you would call a hunch player. She would play certain horses' names, certain numbers, certain jockeys, and believe it or not, her dreams. I do not know what hunch she used that day, but she told my brother and me she had the winning ticket in the first half of the "Twin Double". She asked us what she should do. We told my mom and dad it was their decision, however, if they decided to sell it, we would give them $1,000 for the ticket. We also promised if we should happen to hit the second half, we would give them a nice bonus. My dad thought a bird in the hand was worth two in the bush. My mom agreed and decided to sell us the ticket. So, for the selections in the second half, my brother did the handicapping, and I would exchange the ticket. Excitingly, Duke's selection won the 8th race and now it was time to announce the possible payouts. On our selection, there was only one outstanding ticket, ours, which if our selection won, would be worth $24,000, which was the entire betting pool. Once the payouts were announced, my mom and dad began shaking like a leaf. We were then approached by a regular horseplayer that we knew, and he asked if we wanted to do a saver of $1000. A saver means if our horse wins the race, we will give him $1000 and vice versa. My brother did something that surprised me. He said to me, "you make the call." My dad was telling me to do it, take the saver, but I do not know why I just had this feeling and I told my brother to let it ride. Incredibly, our horse won the 9th race and in my pocket I had a ticket that was worth $24,000. We did not attempt to cash the ticket that day but waited until the next day. We asked our brother-in-law, Dolly's husband Bob if he would want to cash the ticket. We offered him 5% ($1200) and promised to save losing tickets so he could deduct his losses on his tax returns, he agreed.

Back in the '60s, a person who won a lot of money gambling would be able to deduct losing tickets resulting in no money owed to the IRS. Oh yeah, the bonus we gave our parents for selling us the ticket was a brand spanking new Buick Skylark, especially picked out by my mom. As I said, Hollywood could not have written this scenario. Sometimes truth is stranger than fiction.

At this point in time, I was riding high and my plan of becoming a horse trainer had long been forgotten and my dream of being a comedian had faded into oblivion. Shortly after my 20th birthday, January of 1967, my life was about to change dramatically. A group of friends and I went out for the night. We headed out to our favorite dance club; however, when we got there it was closed for no apparent reason. So, one of the guys suggested a new club that had opened, and we should check it out. As we entered the club, there was a table of girls dead ahead and one of them jumped up and yelled "Jody", which was my friend's name. I ran to her and said, "Hey, I'm here" She gave me a snide look and said, "You're not Jody" When she spotted Jody, she invited us to the table. She was totally into him, so I thought I'd move on.

As I got to the table, I noticed a young girl sitting there and introduced myself. My first thought, she was pretty and looked great in her outfit. So, I asked her if she would like to dance. Her name was Carol and she said "yes". We danced a lot that night both fast and slow. During one slow dance, I remembered what Elvis Presley did in one of his movies, so I said to her as we were dancing, "I think I have something in my eye," I pulled my lower lid down and said, "Do you see anything?" She leaned in to take a little closer to look, and I gave her a quick kiss on the lips. I risked a slap in the face, but instead, I got a big laugh.

Now, I had never been in love at that point and I'm not sure if at the time I knew what love was, but I did know that I had a warm feeling dancing and laughing with her and I had never had this feeling before. As the night ended, I asked for her phone number and she willingly gave it to me. I called her the next day and during our conversation, I asked if she would like to go out on a date and she said "yes". She had just broken up with her boyfriend she had been dating since junior high school. It was the first time since the breakup that she decided to date. We started dating and shortly after our first date, we were "going steady."

She came from a dysfunctional family also. Her dad was an alcoholic and was separated from her mom although they never divorced. Her oldest sister married at 16 to a guy in his mid-20's. They got divorced but had a boy and a girl during their marriage. Another older sister got pregnant at a young age, had the child, and then gave it up for adoption. My new girlfriend Carol was 15 months older than me, so at the time we met, she was already 21.

Her family liked me, but I cannot say the same for mine. Of course, she had two strikes against her because my mother thought no one was good enough for her sons. Things were getting serious between us and we both wanted to get out of the house and start a life. Like I stated earlier, I was not sure what love was, but I felt love for her and wanted to spend the rest of my life with her. I believed she loved me as well so we decided to get married in spite of objections of my mother, my dad stayed neutral, and because I was 20 years old I had to threaten my mother with "you'll never see me again" to get her to sign for me which she eventually did. We were married in a judge's home on May 13, 1967. No big wedding, no big honeymoon. My oldest sister Anne and her common law husband Ronnie acted as witnesses. Anne had just purchased another house which she was moving into, so she made the arrangements for us to move into her old apartment.

Things were still going well at the racetrack. I now had a good chunk of cash. We bought new furniture and things were going well. In September of '67, Carol got pregnant. Her family was excited, my side which consists of my mother not so much. On July 24th, 1968, my wife gave birth to our son Edward Anthony. 1968 was the last good year at the racetrack.

Chapter 8

In 1969 things started changing at the New England tracks. There were now three different outfits playing the call and due to many complaints by the fans who were noticing the tote board, which displayed the odds of the horses, would change one last time once the race began and that the odds on a particular horse, which would be the one we "called" would drop sometimes significantly. This led the public to believe something fishy was going on, and although it was perfectly legal, most agreed it was unfair to the other betters so all four of the New England tracks retooled the mutual machines to lock the instant the starting gate opened. What to do now. I was a husband and a father who had to take care of his family. My brother contacted the other "Call Boys" to see if they had any plans. My brother's old partner T.G. who moved to Detroit had come back to Rhode Island and he contacted my brother about other tracks that had an "open bell". Meaning their machines would not lock until half a dozen or so seconds had elapsed. So, T.G., my brother and I began talking road trips to various parts of the country.

It was working well, and we were winning. We played tracks in New Jersey, Pennsylvania, Kentucky, Michigan, Ohio, and even parts of Canada. I kept putting money away, and in that year, my brother gave my youngest sister Antonia (Dolly) $2,000 and I put up $2,000 and we went partners on a two-family house in Johnston, Rhode Island. Duke gave the money to my sister because my brother-in-law, Bob, (Dolly's husband) was the only one who could qualify for a mortgage.

As the New Year rolled around, 1970, things were beginning to unravel. More and more tracks were shutting down their machines at post time. There were fewer and fewer tracks that still had an "open bell".

So, the road trips became few and far between, and by the end of the year and the beginning of 1971, for all intents and purposes, it was over. No more call, no more road trips, what to do now.

After it was finally over, Duke started to hang out with some guys who had their own social club in a predominately Italian area on the other end of Providence. At this point, my brother had just gotten married at which I was the best man. Do not get me wrong, it was at a judge's home and his girlfriend, Michelle who was known as Mickey, was pregnant. She had been divorced and had two small children, a girl, Rachel, 4 years old and a boy David, 2 years old. Although my brother had a hefty amount of cash at the time, he still needed to make money to support his family. At the club, he would shoot crap, play poker, and do whatever to hustle a buck. There were a couple of "wise guys" that hung around and he was introduced to one of them who was well respected and well connected. He invited my brother to stick around and play poker with him. As time went on, they built a relationship. Not long after, my brother became his consigliere. They worked on several "ventures" together, which over the years made my brother a rich man.

This was a highly stressful lifestyle, in which my brother would smoke and drink heavily. After three children together with Mickey, a beautiful home, new cars, their marriage was falling apart. The intense pressure and extreme anxiety of his lifestyle plus the weight of a failing marriage led to my brother's demise. In 1996, he was diagnosed with lung cancer which metastasized to the brain. I would visit my brother almost every day at the hospital. One day when I was there in his room a nurse came in to draw a blood sample; however, she was having an exceedingly difficult time finding the vein. My brother and I became extremely frustrated, then out of nowhere a doctor walks in and says, "let me try". His name was Dr. McKittrick. He instantly found the vein, drew the blood then handed it to the nurse. After the nurse left the room the Dr. said he would like to speak to my brother alone.

After twenty minutes or so had passed; Dr. McKittrick came out of the room and said, "he is ok now". I said to my brother Duke, "wow he is amazing". My brother responded with "more than you know". As Duke and I were talking I noticed a huge difference in his demeanor.

He appeared calmer, relaxed, almost serene. Usually Duke would be agitated, frustrated, almost to a point of anger. I began wondering what was going on here.

Although my brother's hospital stay was gut-wrenching, Dr. McKittrick was always there to soothe him. Duke knew he was terminal, but he seemed to be at peace. The day before he was released, Dr. McKittrick stopped by brother's room. I was there along with my sister in law, Mickey, and my nieces and nephews. I witnessed the doctor in a very spiritual way telling us all that Duke was going to be okay.

He did not mean getting well but I believe he meant that in a Saintly or Godly way. The day my brother was released, Dr. McKittrick was not there. I asked where he was, and the nurse on duty said, "he left for Germany last night". This seemed mysterious to me. Why didn't Dr. McKittrick mention that to us? I feel with every fiber in my body that this doctor was my brother's guardian angel who came to help my brother find peace. Sadly, in March of 1997, my brother passed away.

He was 54 years old. We had some remarkable times together. There were incredible moments I will never forget. He was a huge chapter in my life, and I will never forget him.

I was married with a young child in 1972 and I was, for all intents and purposes, out of work. I could not go back to working in the stable that would not have generated enough money to support my family. Back in those days, it was uncommon for a wife to work and personally I felt that my son would be best served to have his mom 24/7. Maybe back to the stables and a second job of some kind. I still had a healthy amount of cash left to tide me over, but I still needed to generate an income.

I kept thinking about the direction I could head in to and what kind of job opportunities would be available to me. Never, not even for a fleeting moment did I even think about being a comedian. One day I stopped by the neighborhood luncheonette. This was a place where a lot of the guys from our corner would hang around. I bumped into my brother's old friend Bernie. We chatted for a while and eventually, he asked what I was doing now. He knew my brother and I was playing the races. I told him it was over, and the "call" could no longer be played. He asked about my brother and I told him he was hanging at a social club. He asked me what I was going to do to make a living. I told him I was not sure. Bernie drove a truck for a heating oil company and would get laid off every summer. He had just gotten laid off, and I asked what he was going to do for the summer. He said he was collecting unemployment and that he started working under the table for a local guy he knew from the neighborhood named Peter, who had a used car lot. Bernie's job was to drive Peter's cars to and from the auctions as well as pick up and deliver sales and purchases.

As the conversation continued, Bernie came up with an idea: He proposed that if I would put up the cash, we could buy cars from Peter at a wholesale price and resell them out of our yards and through newspaper ads. He guaranteed me that we would get the cars at a low enough price that we would easily make a profit. I thought for a moment that this would only be temporary, but I could make some money until I could find something permanent. So, I agreed to the deal. I put up the initial capital and we started our business. We bought several cars off Peter and in a matter of a couple of weeks; we sold a few of them at a healthy profit. Bernie started to get over-excited and we bought a lot of cars and had them all over the place. Both our yards were now packed with cars and we even had cars on the street with For Sale signs in the window.

Cars were selling well, and we were making money. This went on through most of the summer. Late that summer we sold a car to a guy who suffered some mechanical problems with the car he bought and, instead of calling us, he went to the police. The cops came to both our houses, saw all the cars, and told us, in no uncertain terms, that we needed to give the buyer his money back and stop selling immediately or we would be charged with operating a business without a license. We complied. And that was the end of that business.

The problem now was I had no job, over a dozen cars, and nowhere to sell them, plus Bernie got called back to work. Now here I am stuck with these cars, what could I do? A few days later and no job in sight, Bernie called me and said he talked to Peter, who would be willing to help me sell the cars. So, Bernie set up a time for us to meet. The next day I went to meet Peter and explained everything, and what cars I had left. He agreed to take the cars to the auto auction and sell them for me. He told me the cars would be sold at auction prices and I probably would not make any money, just hopefully get my investment back. I told him I would be happy just to get my money back and I would be okay with even a small loss if necessary. Now I had never been to a car auction, so this would be all new to me.

For the next couple of weeks, I attended several auctions and watched my cars being sold. I found the whole process extremely interesting. Finally, the last car got sold. After all the expenses, I had approximately $4,000 in Peter's account. Which was fine because I had approximately $4,000 invested in all the cars. A couple of days later I met with Peter again to settle up. He said, "Before I write you this check, how would you like to go to work for me?" I was surprised. I said, "Doing what?" He said, "As my buyer." I said, "I don't really know how to buy cars". He said, "You did it before, putting cars in the newspaper." I said, "You were telling us what to buy." He said, "That's what you would do for me. Let me explain, you drive out to as many new car dealers as you can in a day and ask the sales manager if he or she has any cars they want to wholesale. If they do, you look at the cars, then call me and describe them to me and how much they are asking, and I will let you know if you should buy them. The deal is you use your money to buy them, I'll clean them and get them ready for the auction sale, and we split the profits 50-50 after expenses"

I think subconsciously I knew accepting this deal would once and for all bury my dreams forever. I was about to embark on a career that would generate a solid income, but one that was going to cause pain, heartache, shame, and misery, for years to come. I accepted the offer and started my career as an auto buyer. What I did not know was getting the car ready entailed rolling back the odometer.

I never really wanted to be in the car business. It was not something I thought about or dreamed about. I got into it by necessity.

When I had all the cars I purchased with Bernie I had to sell them, so when I was approached by Peter with his offer, I felt I had no choice but to except. I admit it was exciting in the beginning but quickly it got old. The everyday ordeal of driving from dealer to dealer all over New England, then the chore of getting the cars ready, spending the entire day at the auction, and then selling them became a 60-70-hour week endeavor. Add to that, and this is not sour grapes, but the other dealers you had to deal with did not have extremely high moral standards. Other dealers would sell you out at any opportunity. If you had a new car dealer you bought from on a regular basis it was called "your stop". Most (not all) used car dealers would go to your stop and try to undermine your relationship and even offer to undercut your offers. To put it bluntly, used car dealers were mostly backstabbing, conniving, careless characters who would do almost anything to make a buck.

I am not trying to take the moral high ground here, because I was right in the mix of all this and it is something I am not proud of, to say the least. I am certainly remorseful and regretful I ever got into the business.

Granted, I was making good money, which made it hard to walk away from. But, as I reflect on those days, I realize how foolish and gullible I was.

I thought I was a big deal when, in fact, I was nothing but a phony who was breaking the law to make a good living.

Chapter 9

I remember one night I was running late at the auction, so I called Carol to let her know. she said, "Duke" and his wife Mickey have invited me to go out to dinner with them". Would you mind if I go"?

I told her I didn't mind, and I would see her when I got home. I arrived home from the auction around 8:30 pm and ate some leftovers and started watching television. I recall falling asleep on the couch when the phone rang. I checked my watch and it was a little after 2:00 am so I did not think this call was going to be good. I was right. It was my brother Duke who was hysterical with emotion. He said, "there was an accident, and everyone was at the hospital".

Carol had dropped off our son Ed at my mother in laws house to spend the night, so I immediately rushed to the hospital. When I arrived, I was greeted by my brother who was sobbing, and Mickey was also in tears. I demanded to speak with a doctor. Almost immediately a doctor approached and told me my wife had fractured her skull and would stay in the hospital to be observed and tested for any brain damage. I became furious with my brother and his wife and yelled, "How could you let something like this happen?" They explained through their tears that they all had a few drinks and as they reached my brother's house where Carol's car was, both Mickey and my wife for some ungodly reason hopped on the trunk of my brother's car and said, "give us a ride". My brother got in the car and slammed down the accelerator causing both girls to fly off the trunk on to the pavement. Mickey escaped with minor bruises; However, Carol was not so lucky. She lay on the pavement unconscious. That is when my brother really lost it and began crying uncontrollably, blaming himself and vowing if Carol does not recover, he would kill himself. Fortunately,

Carol made a full recovery, with the exception of losing her sense of smell. I recall vividly the brain surgeon telling me when I first arrived at the hospital; he wasn't worried about the box but the candy inside. What a compelling analogy, thankfully the candy stayed intact.

I bought cars with Peter for several years and then I branched out on my own, buying freelance for other dealers as well as for myself. In 1978, I was sitting in the cafeteria of the auction when a dealer I had seen around but didn't really know approached me and asked if he could sit down. I said, "have a seat". We chatted for several minutes and as we were leaving he asked if I would like to meet him for lunch the following day. He suggested we meet at his car lot in Johnston R.I. I agreed. We had a pleasant lunch talking about cars in general and the car business in particular. then he said, "Before I drop you off, do you mind if I stop by my house for a minute."

Now, I did not know much about him, only knowing his name was Ernie and seeing him at auctions and at some dealers, so it seemed a little strange that he wanted to go out of his way before dropping me off. Why he would want to stop by his house for a minute? The restaurant was a short distance from his car lot. I was a little caught off guard, but I went along with it. We headed toward Lincoln, Rhode Island, which is an exclusive area with many very expensive homes. When we arrived at his house, I had an Idea why. I thought he was out to impress me, and he did just that. We pulled into the driveway of an impeccably landscaped contemporary home, complete with a swimming pool and cabana. The interior of the home was exquisite. It appeared to be professionally decorated. To say I was impressed would be a gross understatement. I now understand why he wanted me to see his house. He introduced me to his wife Eileen, who was decked out and resembled Susan Lucci. We sat down and he got right down to business. He mentioned he was tired of the road and was looking for a buyer. His next move literally floored me. He presented me with an offer. I was taken by surprise, but I listened. He stated, I would buy the cars, using his money, that would be put into an unlimited buyers account and after expenses of getting the cars auction ready, as well as transportation and auction fees, we would have a 50-50 split on all profits from my purchases. It was a generous offer. I sat there for a moment then I told him I had a few loose ends to tie up before I could accept but if the offer still stands in two weeks I would gladly take it. He assured that it would. I sold the few cars I had, explained to the dealers that I would be working exclusively for Ernie from Greenville Motors. This happened in 1978.

Back on the home front, things were not going so well. At approximately the five-year mark of our marriage, 1972, Carol swallowed a bottle of sleeping pills. She had gone to bed and I stayed up watching TV. When I finally went to bed, I realized that something was not right. Generally, she would feel me getting in bed and roll over. However, when I got in bed she did not budge. I tried to say goodnight, but I got no response. Now I tried to wake her, but she did not respond. I suddenly assumed what happened. I called for an ambulance; there was no 9-1-1 back then. While waiting for help, I tried to wake her repeatedly but to no avail. When the emergency team arrived, they quickly took her to the ambulance and rushed her to the hospital.

I called my mother-in-law and told her what happened and asked if she would watch my son so I could get to the hospital. Of course, she complied. After dropping my son off and promising my mother-in-law to let her know what was going on, I zoomed to the hospital. By the time I got to the hospital and to the room where Carol was, she was groggy but awake and coherent. I talked to the doctor who told me that they pumped her stomach and she really did not take enough to kill herself. He said it was more a cry for help and suggested some counseling.

When I questioned my wife on why she would do something like this, she confessed she had been having an affair with her old boyfriend and was so embarrassed and ashamed of herself, she wanted to die. Now normally, being Italian and having that Italian machismo attitude that would have been the end of our marriage. But for me, I just could not bear the idea of another man raising my son. So, I told my wife I still loved her, and I forgive her, and we will work it out. Things were normal for the next few years.

After the car debacle, Bernie and I became close friends. As I mentioned, I was a boxing fan and I found out that Bernie loved boxing as well. So, we started attending local boxing matches in Rhode Island and Massachusetts. As we were attending these matches, we got friendly with some of the local promoters, and managers as well as several fighters. One up and coming boxer we were following was a young man named Marvin Hagler. He was trained and managed by the Petronelli Brothers.

Pat Petronelli acted as his manager and Goody Petronelli was Marvin's trainer. The Pertronelli Brothers had a boxing gym in Brockton, Massachusetts that featured a stable of boxers including Goody's son Tony Petronelli. As Bernie and I kept attending the local fights we got friendly with Goody who ran the gym and we asked if it would be okay to come by to watch his fighters train. Goody was gracious and said it would be fine. Bernie and I would visit the gym once or twice a month and noticed how Marvin Hagler's career was blossoming. As we watched Marvin fight and train it was obvious, he was something special. Bernie and I would attend as many of the Hagler fights as possible cheering on the "Champ" As our relationship with Goody became friendlier he felt comfortable enough to allow us in the dressing room on fight night. We were there for many of Hagler's fights, even a Championship bout, which took place in Atlantic City on March 7, 1982, in which Hagler knocked out William "Caveman" Lee in the first round. I myself would even spend time at Marv's training camp in Provincetown, Massachusetts. It was an exciting and special time to be so close to a sports legend. And to boot, the "Champ" was a super nice guy. I have so many great memories.

In 1976, Bernie and I drove to New York in an attempt to see Muhamad Ali fight Ernie Shavers at Yankee Stadium. We did not have any tickets. We just thought we would get there and find scalpers, or someone who had extra tickets or somehow try to weasel our way in. We arrived at the Stadium eager to get a seat at the fight. We approached a turnstile where an attendant was stationed. We told him we wanted to see the fight but did not have any tickets and asked where we can get a couple. He said, "Give me twenty bucks."

We did and he let us through.

Less than thirty feet away an NYPD officer came up to us and said, "Come here, I saw what you did". Now I am thinking we are going to jail. What he said next shocked me. He said, "Why didn't you give it to me?" He went on to say, "you guys want to get in the infield"? We said, "we'd love it". He said, "give me twenty", which we did, and he then escorted us down to the sixth row from the ring. When we settled in our seats, we noticed many celebrities in the crowd. I saw Telly Savalas, Ella Fitzgerald,

Brent Musburger, among others. I also noticed a young Sugar Ray Leonard who just returned from the Montreal Olympics and was wearing his gold medal. I approached him and congratulated him, and he was very gracious. What a thrill! It was an amazing night watching Muhammed Ali who I believe was the greatest fighter of all time. Sorry, Dad!!

Chapter 10

The 1980s were without a doubt the darkest years of my life, but with a massive silver lining. By 1980 I had been working with Ernie for two years making good money and although we were rolling back odometers, he assured me if anything came down, he would take the heat. Also, that year, Carol decided she wanted to go to work. At that time, she had nice clothes, fine jewelry, a new car, a beautiful home. And I felt she really did not need to work. I say this with no animosity whatsoever but she had no higher education or any special skills so I assumed she would only get a menial job. Remember, this was the early 1980's. I certainly would not have felt that way today. She insisted and I said, "if you want it that badly, I'm okay with it". She got a job as a waitress at a Greek Restaurant.

One night she came home from work and her car had been splattered with raw eggs. The next morning, I asked what happened and she said one of the other waitresses were jealous of her. It sounded fishy to me. Also, she was staying later and later at the restaurant because she just wanted to help her boss get ready for the next day. I said to her "I think something funny is going on at work, and I think you should let me know what is happening." She assured me nothing was going on.

One night, after going out to dinner, history repeated itself. With my mother-in-law there at our house staying over after watching my son, my wife took another bottle of sleeping pills. Once again, I rushed her to the hospital and this time her reasoning was a little different. She was pregnant. Now, I am not a detective, but by all indications, I believe I know who was responsible. My wife demanded an abortion on the grounds that ingesting the pills could cause a birth defect. I was devastated. However, at this point, my son was 12 years old and I certainly did not want to have his teenage years shaped by another man. So, once again, this time reluctantly I forgave her. She quit her job and we were a family again.

On the work side, I found out that Ernie was being investigated by the Rhode Island Attorney General for odometer fraud. Something I did not know at the time I started working for him. I was upset about it and he assured me that after several meetings with the Attorney General's office, he negotiated a cease and desist agreement that he would never do it again, in exchange for a no conviction, fine, or any penalties under law. Sounded like a sweet deal. However, there was a problem. He could not stop. He was living a rich man's lifestyle, and if he quit, he would more than likely lose most of it. Besides, he had a high style wife who loved the finer things in life, and he feared if he stopped, he might lose her too.

Let me add that I was doing very well financially, and due to my greed and stupidity I did not walk away.

So, Ernie called a meeting with me and explained he concocted a plan. instead of running the other way, foolishly I said, "I'm in". The plan was laid out as follows. Ernie had a cousin, Angelo, who owned a body shop with a dealer's license. Angelo met with Ernie earlier and they worked out a deal where Ernie would pay Angelo $100 for every car sold at the auction win or lose. And if anything came down, Ernie would take the heat. Angelo agreed and things returned to business as usual.

There were automobile titles in 1980's, so getting a title for a vehicle without the actual mileage filled in on the title was difficult. One day a local dealer who Ernie knew had stopped by the car lot to talk to Ernie. He told him he was running an operation where he would drive down to North Carolina and register a bunch of cars at their DMV and receive a brand-new North Carolina title with the lower altered mileage on it, and if Ernie were interested he would do it for $150 per title. Ernie went ahead and agreed without telling his cousin Angelo. This scheme went on for quite a while until so many applications were being put through the North Carolina DMV that it prompted an investigation.

In 1983, Ernie's cousin Angelo came by the lot with a letter stating that he was being investigated for the alteration of fraudulent documents. He was outraged. He confronted Ernie and demanded he clear his name as to their agreement. Within days we had all gotten the same letter. Ernie, Ernie's brother Kenny who worked as lot manager and myself. We all lawyered up. We were summoned to appear in court in North Carolina. I had never flown in my life up to that point and had a fear of it. So, a day earlier I boarded a train.

Ernie hired one of the finest lawyer's money could buy out of Boston and he was the lead attorney. Our first day in court, the prosecution was looking for some serious jail time. The lawyers had a meeting that night after court. After their meeting, they came up with a defense which they were going to present the following day. Remember the charge was fraudulent documents, so the defense team brilliantly defended that just because the odometer reading was different than the mileage on the car, the title i.e. document was still the same, and they showed an example. Ernie's lawyer held up the title of a 1980 Cadillac. He argued that the mileage on the back does not change the document. It is still a 1980 Cadillac with the exact same serial number. The judge gave the prosecution a strong reprimand and said quote, "You sold the farm" and with that, he adjourned until the next morning.

The next day in court the prosecution made a futile attempt to bolster their case but to no avail. The judge dropped the fraudulent document charge; however, he did charge us with odometer tampering and sentenced us to serve time in a halfway house in Massachusetts. Ernie and I got four months, his brother Kenny and his cousin Angelo got two months each. What could have been a long prison term was reduced to a short stay at a halfway house thanks to some crafty legal work by our team of attorneys.

1983 remained a bad year; One morning my dad, who was working for me after he retired, did not show up for work. Being a former taxi driver, I hired him to pick up and deliver cars to dealers and auctions. I called my mom to see if everything was alright and she told me my dad had fallen and his left leg was numb. After work, I met my brother Duke at my mom's house to check on my dad. We asked what happened and he said his leg just gave out. My dad had been healthy his whole life, he never was hospitalized or even sick with the flu. So, my brother and I thought we should get to the bottom of it. We reluctantly convinced him to get checked by a doctor.

After several tests and x-rays, it was determined my dad had a brain tumor. The medical team wanted to meet the family. My mom was against meeting them as she still festered the opinion that it was the surgeons that killed my brother Sonny. So, it fell upon my brother and my shoulders to meet with the medical team. We were told in the meeting that my father indeed had a malignant brain tumor, but the good news was that it was very operable and with my dad's current good health, they were confident it could be removed, and my dad could have many years left.

We took this news back to my mom and she went into this wild scenario of my dad becoming a vegetable and who will take care of him. She said she could not do it and she said, "Remember what happened to my son"? Now I also remember my dad saying, "If you get a splinter you need to get it out." We told them to talk it over. The next night we met again at my mom's house and my dad said he wasn't going to go through with the operation and recovery, it would be too much, and he stated that he would be happy with one more baseball season. To this day I believe if my mom had given him her approval, he would have had the operation. But because he loved her so much, he stood by her decision. Unfortunately, my dad did not make another baseball season. He passed away in March of 1984.

He was 78 years old.

At this point, my marriage was now a total failure. We had a beautiful house, my wife drove a brand-new car, but it was a cold home. I knew many years earlier that my goal was to stay until my son reached the age of 18. Then I would file for divorce. I felt terrible about divorcing my wife because on her own she would surely lose her lifestyle. Or maybe because I still loved her. Because of those reasons I decided to give it one more try. This is crazy, but we sold our house and bought a brand new bigger one and traded her brand-new Cougar for a brand-new sports car, a Toyota MR2. Things went well for a while, until she decided she wanted an open marriage. I thought this idea was crazy, but I also thought that I would let her have it because maybe it would bring her back, but it did not. In fact, it went straight to her having men pick her up at our house.

This was really the final straw. I moved out, we sold the house and we both agreed to start divorce proceedings. We agreed to a 50-50 split of all monetary assets, plus the new furniture, and the new car would all go to her. We were officially divorced in 1986 just around the time my son turned 18 years old. After the divorce, I found out she had moved in with our refrigerator repairman, who she had been having an affair with, to the best of my knowledge, for a year or so.

In late 1984 Ernie's brother, Kenny, was going to be married and Ernie was planning a bachelor party for him and invited me. I told him I really did not like bachelor parties, because I didn't drink and thought the whole thing was kind of juvenile. Ernie explained that this one would be different because there would be no strippers or other working women, but that Ernie had hired two professional comedians from a local comedy club called Periwinkles that had just opened up in downtown Providence. I did not want to go at first, but there was something inside of me: was it a voice, a feeling, a twinge? I cannot explain, but everything inside me was telling me you have to go.

The party was being held in a banquet room in a local restaurant. The show started with the first comedian, Ed Del Grande, coming out. He did some comedy material and some juggling. He performed for approximately 30 minutes, and then he introduced the next comic and left the stage to a warm round of applause. The second comedian, Frank O'Donnell, was a heavy-set guy with an edgy attitude. He did some comedy and then started working the audience like a poor man's Don Rickles. He was getting off some good lines and because of his insults of others in attendance, the crowd was roaring. Suddenly he picked on me. He began with some friendly insults about my apparel. I shot back with some quips of my own. This went on for several minutes and then he decided to move on.

After he completed his show, he went to the bar. While he was enjoying a soft drink, I felt compelled to go over and talk to him. I praised him for his show and told him I really enjoyed our back and forth banter. What I said next just came out without me thinking of anything. It was not premeditated, I had no agenda, I wasn't even thinking at that time of my life about being a comedian. Remember, my dream was dead and buried. But what I said next was not only life-changing but also a death knell to my old life. The Ed Regine that I was at that time would be dead forever. I would be reborn as a completely new person. I can't explain what happened next. Was it an epiphany, my guardian angel, a spirit, I don't know? All I remember is very casually saying, "I always wanted to be a comedian." I surprised myself by what I said. It just came out. I expected a mild response. I assumed he would say something like, "that's nice" or "really?" Instead, he said "well if you ever want to try, I have an open mic night on Thursdays at Periwinkles". I was stunned. My only reply was

"Periwinkles"? I felt my heart jump into my throat. I got this indescribable feeling of euphoria and immediately blurted out "I'd love to." He said he was booked for the upcoming week but if I wanted, he would give me a five-minute spot on the following week. I said "Yes!"

At the beginning of 1985, at the tender age of 38, I made my very first standup comedy appearance. Leading up to that first spot, I was extremely nervous. First of all, I had no real material; I really didn't know how to figure out what to say. I thought about it and I finally came up with an idea to use some of the silly things I have said in the past. I decided right from the start to not have any of my friends or family come see me until I was good enough not to embarrass them. I did tell my wife, but she did not show much interest due to the fact that we were on the verge of divorce.

Chapter 11

The big night came, and I was a nervous wreck. I could not stop thinking about not doing well and getting booed off the stage. I had cobbled together a few jokes about my large nose, about being Italian, Italian girls, and reciting the opening to the old Superman TV show backwards. It was something I learned as a kid and it stuck in my brain all these years. As I watched the other comedians while waiting for my turn, I could tell most of them had experience and it showed. This only heightened my thoughts of bombing.

Frank O'Donnell, from the bachelor party, and his partner, Charlie Hall were there. Frank and Charlie both were responsible for booking comedians at Periwinkles. Frank was hosting the show that night and came to me and said, "You're up next." That put my adrenaline glands into overdrive. He said, "When you see me standing here, that means you have one-minute left." And he headed for the stage. The rest of it was a blur. I heard him say my name and I walked out on the stage. It was a small room. It held approximately 125 people and it was at best half full. I nervously went into my routine, and amazingly people were laughing.

There are no words to describe my feeling. I don't think there is a drug on this planet that could give me the sensation I was feeling at that moment. I was hooked. After a minute or two, it became crystal clear to me that this is what I was born to do. I looked over at the spot where Frank would stand, and he was not there. I was out of material. I just said thank you and goodnight to the audience.

I was in the back of the room pacing and trying to compose myself when, after introducing the next comic, Frank came over to me and asked, "How do you feel?" I said, "I'm speechless"." He asked if I was nervous up there and I said "Very." He replied, "Well you looked comfortable. Would you like to come back next week?" I answered "Absolutely?" He said, "Okay, you're on the show next week."

As I was walking to my car, so many thoughts were flying around in my brain. I had this feeling for the first time in my life of being somebody, doing something important. Again, it was truly a feeling of being free. Free from the past and on my way to a brand-new life. But shaking the past was more than a daunting task. After my first open mic, I could not wait for the next week to come. After several open mics, I started to attend as many of the weekend comedy shows as possible. I could not stay away, I had to be there. To watch, to listen, to absorb as much as I could. This was now my passion, lust, craving, desire, and yearning, all of it. Comedy was now my life, my heart, my soul.

One night at Periwinkles, some weeks after my first open mic, I watched a Boston comic named Rich Ciesler. He was the headliner for that particular weekend. The headliners who came to Providence were mostly Boston comedians and, occasionally, a Connecticut or New York comic. Rich rattled off a blistering 45-minute set and the audience loved it. Basically "He Killed." As I was watching this consummate pro, I thought to myself, there is no way I am ever going to be that good and have that much material. But little by little, I developed more material and after several weeks I had approximately 10 minutes of decent material. Each Thursday I was there to do my act and try to squeeze in a new bit or two. Then, on weekends, I would be at Periwinkles to watch and study.

In April of 1985, with approximately 15-20 minutes of decent material, I got my first paid gig at Periwinkles, the place where I did my first open mic. Frank's partner, comedian Charlie Hall, asked me if I would like to host next weekend's shows: two shows Friday, two shows Saturday for a total of $50. I nearly jumped out of my skin and said "yes". At this early stage of my career Charlie Hall had begun taking me under his wing. I would go with Charlie to his shows on the road and watch and study. Charlie was funny, clever and very entertaining, all done in a silly kind of way. He was also immensely helpful in my career. After my weekend gig which went well, but I was not killing, Frank O'Donnell had set up a showcase at a comedy club in the Boston area. The audition was for a major Boston booking agent, Barry Katz, who booked talent for Play It Again

Sam's which was a popular comedy club in the basement of a restaurant in Allston Massachusetts. I did the showcase there and it went fine. The next day Frank called me and asked if it went well. I said, "I think so." "Well, he said Barry thought you were a little rough around the edges but was willing to give you a shot". I was more than elated. I was feeling on top of the world. More and more I knew that this is what I was meant to do.

Not long after my showcase, perhaps several weeks, I received a call from Charlie Hall, who told me that Barry's wife had passed away. The news was shocking. She was in her mid-twenties; the cause of death was anorexia. I had only met Barry a couple of times at Play It Again Sam's, so I hardly knew him. Frank and Charlie asked if I wanted to attend the wake with them. Like I said I barely knew Barry and I had never met his wife but again something inside me made me want to go. As I was going down the receiving line, I reached Barry and for whatever reason, I felt this strong bond that was happening as we were clenched together in a prolonged hug. That embrace was the beginning of a friendship that has lasted for decades.

Several months after the funeral, my phone rings. It was Barry Katz. He asked if I was available the upcoming Saturday. Of course, I said "yes". He told me I would open for a Boston comedy team called Zito and Bean at John Martin's Manor, a restaurant in Waterville Maine. John Martin incidentally was the brother of Andrea Martin of SCTV fame. The pay was $125. I had to pick the team up in Boston and drive to the gig, stay overnight in a hotel and drive them back to Boston the next day. I was walking on air. I felt like I had already made it in the world of comedy.

Barry had his office in his house in Allston, Massachusetts so occasionally when I had a gig in the area I would pop in. The very first time I stopped by, I was shocked and saddened by what I saw. Still, after many months, Barry had his wife's clothes hanging in the closet, the table set for dinner, and "I love you Honey" written in lipstick on the bathroom mirror. He seemed so depressed. I felt like I had to do something. I suggested that any off Monday I had I would drive to his office and we would go out to dinner and take in a movie. After some friendly persuasion, he agreed. Thus, the transition started.

As I was still working on my act, one night at Periwinkles a professional comedian named Steve O, who was headlining that night, came to me and said, "You know, you look like a lot of characters and you should do them in your act." He mentioned Klinger from MASH, Murray the Cop, Al from Happy Days, so I thought maybe it could work. I took his advice and went out and bought a hairnet with curlers, a police hat, and a short-order cook hat. The next time on stage I pulled them out and put them on my head and just said the name and the audience went wild. Wow, I had no idea it would work so well. So, that inspired me to come up with more characters. I came up with the Native American who stood by the side of the road with litter at his feet and a tear rolling down his cheek. I also bought, besides the Native American wig, a soft hat, sunglasses, and a string mop, and did ZZ Top. The audience was going wild.

Then I took it to the next level. I had been closing my show with an impression of Tina Turner ordering a pizza. One night at Play It Again Sam's, where I showcased for Barry Katz, I was doing a guest set and when I went into the Tina Turner impression, one audience member yelled out "What about the legs?" and the entire audience was yelling, "Yeah! Yeah!" So, I thought for a second and did the unthinkable, I dropped my pants. The crowd went bonkers. The laughter was deafening.

As I was driving home, I thought what if I went all the all with the Tina Turner impression. I decided to go for it. I purchased three wigs, a jean skirt, fishnet stockings and tubes of red Lipstick. Here is what I came up with: I would be on stage, and then I would call two guys up from the audience to don wigs and back me up as the Ikettes. I would be wearing tear away sweatpants and have the Tina outfit underneath.

The song Proud Mary would be playing and during the slow part of the song, I would put wigs on myself and the guys and apply the lipstick, turn around and dance slowly. When the song came to the part where it speeds up, I would remove my pants to unveil the skirt and fishnets, and then the house would come down.

After a while of doing this in my act, none of Boston or Rhode Island comics could follow me I was now making my mark as a headliner. Barry knew about this as he was the one booking me on these shows and because we had a close relationship, he was always there to aid me in my career. This caused quite a stir in the Boston comedy community. Boston comics telling Barry how he could book someone doing the things on stage that

I was doing, Barry said "of all the comedians who work all of my comedy rooms, (and he had over 30) Ed is far and away the most requested".

It was a hot July night as I was driving back from a gig on Route 128 in Massachusetts. Suddenly a Massachusetts state trooper lights me up and pulls me over. He said I had a taillight out and he was going to give me three days to repair it. Resting on the front seat next to me was my little prop suitcase. So, the trooper was curious and asked what was in the suitcase. I told him I was a comedian and my props were in there. He asked if he could look and I said "sure". I opened it and revealed wigs for my Tina Turner bit plus all the other props for my various characters. He asked about the wigs and fishnets and I told him that I use them for my Tina Turner impression. He then shocked me when he said, "Can you show me?" So right then and there on route 128 at approximately 11:00 pm, I did my Tina Turner impression. When I finished, he handed me back my paperwork and said, "Get that light fixed." What came next really surprised me when he said "Oh, and don't quit your day job."

In November of 1985 Barry asked if I would attend Thanksgiving dinner with him and his in-laws. Because my marriage was in shambles, I accepted. The holidays were rough for both Barry and me. As 1986 rolled around, I was still working out at the Rhode Island club and getting paid gigs throughout New England, including clubs, colleges, and corporate events. For the next several years I was performing approximately 300 shows a year.

Chapter 12

In the spring of 1988, I got a call from Barry Katz. He informs me that he hooked up with an entertainment agency on the island of Bermuda who wanted a comedian for one of their venues.

Barry asked if I wanted to do it.

It would be a two-week contract and at that point in my life, I knew Bermuda was an island, however, I wasn't sure exactly where it was located. My first question to Barry was "how do I get there?" He said, "you would fly there". Up to this point in my life, I had never been on an airplane, mostly due to fear that I had, and compounded by my brother Duke who had flown several times and swore he would never do it again. I asked my brother what it was like and he said it feels like the top of your head is coming off. That was the clincher and I decided I was never going to get on an airplane. So, my next question for Barry was, "Can I take a boat there?" Barry said, "look if you are going to have a career in this business you are going to need to fly". I told him I could not do it. After much back and forth on the issue, Barry then said, "will you do it if I go with you?" I knew Barry was right. If I wanted this bad enough, I would have to fly. I said, "OK, I'll do it if you fly with me". He promised he would and arranged our flights. We would be flying on Delta Airlines from Boston to Philadelphia and then Philly to Bermuda. We met at Barry's office and headed to Logan Airport. We boarded the plane, took our seats, mine was a window and I sat gripping my armrests with all my might. I was the poster boy for a white knuckler. As the plane took off, I noticed it was smooth, nothing like my brother described. I remember refusing to lift my window shade but then I started to relax a little as we reached cruising altitude because the flight was so smooth.

The next thing I know there was a thud that startled me. That is when Barry said, "We just landed!" The flight was one of the smoothest flights I have ever been on and I thought to myself, this is what I was so afraid of? As we were leaving the plane, I said to a male flight attendant, was my first plane ride and I'm shocked on how smooth it was". He replied, "that it is about as good as it gets". As of this writing, for someone who was petrified to fly, I have flown a little over one and a half million miles in my career. We landed in Bermuda and headed to our hotel called "The Bermudiana."

The venue was within walking distance from the hotel. It was in downtown Hamilton in a lounge named the "Forty Thieves'. We got there on opening night and met the booking agent Tony Brennen. He was well known on the island as the go-to guy for entertainment.

Tony had booked a variety type show with local talent, a band from Barbados, and me. Opening night went great and Tony and Barry seemed incredibly pleased. Tony set us up with mopeds so we could tool around the island. Bermuda is, without question, a gorgeous paradise. Barry and I had a great time spending our days at the beach and nights at the club. After the first week, Barry headed back to Boston while I would stay and finish out the contract. One morning I get a call from Tony who invited me to a lawn party and BBQ at the home of Robert Stigwood, a famous producer who created "Hair" and "Jesus Christ Superstar". That was an incredible afternoon. To give you an example of how influential Tony Brennan was, Robert Stigwood was out of town on the day of the party but gave the keys to his multi-million-dollar estate to Tony to throw a party for his entertainers. About ten days into the contract I got another call from Barry telling me that Tony wants to hold me over for one more week. I agreed to do it. One night at the club something amazing happened. Remember this was 1988 and I was still using props in my act and always closing with the Tina Turner impression. On one particular night I called up two guys from the audience to be my Ikettes.

I put the wigs on them, and the crowd is going wild. As I am prancing around to the music of Proud Mary my Ikettes are doing their thing and the crowd is hysterical. The bit is over, and we get a standing ovation. After the show, I was told that one of the gentlemen I called up on stage was the Premier of the Island of Bermuda, Sir John Swan. The next morning on the front page of the Royal Gazette was a picture of me and the "Ikettes".

I once had a copy of that newspaper article but somehow over the years, it got lost in the shuffle. Performing on cruise ships has brought me back to Bermuda on many occasions and several times I have gone to the library to look at microfilm to find that article but to no avail, however, I will keep trying.

One interesting thing happened during my contract. A cruise ship was overnighting in the town of Hamilton. That evening after my show I was approached by a guy who introduced himself as Buddy Greco. Buddy was a popular vocalist in the '50s, '60s, and '70s, who happened to be performing on that particular cruise ship that was overnighting in port. We exchanged pleasantries and then he said he was going to be performing at Resorts International in Atlantic City and if I would be interested in being his opening act.

I said "yes, I would". He handed me his business card and said get in touch with me when you get back. I said "OK." When I returned home, I called Buddy, unfortunately he told me that he was having a problem with Resort's contract and was trying to work out the issues but to no avail. Buddy eventually told me the gig was not happening. I was disappointed but I felt good about the fact that a national headlining act at a major venue thought enough of my act to want me to open for him. I thought that the fact I had only been doing comedy for a short period of time was quite an accomplishment. Reflecting on my time with Tony Brennen and the Forty Thieves gig, I was thinking after only three years of doing standup comedy, I'm headlining on the Island of Bermuda, being invited to the estate of a world-famous producer, and being asked to be the opening act of a recording artist in a showroom in Atlantic City. The entire thought process was overwhelming. My long lost and forgotten dream is coming to fruition.

Finally, as 1988 ended and 1989 began, the word came out that Ernie was to be indicted. I freaked out. I immediately met with him and asked if this was true. He said, "yes it's true." Ernie, myself, his brother, Kenny, and Cousin Angelo, plus other dealers— eleven in total— were indicted for odometer rollback and mail fraud, which was a federal offense. We were charged with mail fraud because the cars and the paperwork crossed state lines. We all pled guilty and a court date was set for sentencing.

Several months later, at the sentencing, I pleaded with the judge. I begged his forgiveness; I apologized to anyone who was hurt by my actions. I explained I had started a new career and turned my life around. I offered to make full restitution and do whatever community service he would dole out. I once again stated how deeply sorry I was for my actions and behavior regarding this matter. I furthermore explained how I had given my time and talent to charities and fundraising events for many worthy causes. I also submitted to the court many letters of recommendation from various prominent people in my life.

Judge Boyle said "I know you've done some good work and I appreciate that you have made strides in turning your life around. However, this activity has been going on for a long time and it's time to put a stop to it." He then sentenced me to eighteen months in a federal facility. The judge gave me credit for the four months I served in the halfway house, thus reducing my prison time to fourteen months. He also levied a fine of $25,000. As the ringleader, Ernie received a 3-year sentence and a $150,000 fine. Kenny and Angelo were sentenced to probation. I was devastated. I knew what I was doing was wrong, but I never dreamed it would come to this.

Chapter 13

It has been three weeks and I am still struggling with the reality of being in prison. Let us go back to Day One: My sister Anne, Ronnie, her common law husband, Felicia and I jumped into my sister's car bright and early on Monday April 24th, 1989 a day before I was to report to the facility. It was a long arduous drive. We finally arrived in a small town called Ebensburg at approximately 9:00 P.M. We checked in to a somewhat seedy motel, grabbed a quick bite at a fast-food restaurant and retired to our rooms. The night was uneventful as we all were exhausted, and we said goodnight and went to sleep.

We woke around 10:00 A.M on April 25th, Coincidently, the same date my brother "Sonny" had passed away. We had a quick breakfast at a greasy spoon near our motel. I was ordered to report to the facility at noon, however I was curious and anxious to see the institution before I had to report. We arrived there at around 11:15 A.M. and drove around the outer perimeter of the facility which was located in Loretto, Pennsylvania, which is approximately six miles from Ebensburg. It was a former monastery nestled in the hills of Cambria County Pennsylvania. This may sound ridiculous, but it seemed peaceful and serene. As we got closer I noticed the place had the look of a factory or even perhaps a high school. It certainly was not what you would expect a prison to look like. There weren't any fences, walls, or guard towers. The grounds were well groomed and neatly landscaped. I noticed several men were working on what seemed to be a landscaping project. I got a different feeling of what I was expecting. It relieved some of my fears and trepidation. At approximately 11:45 A.M. I was ready to go in. The four of us were escorted to a small holding area and I was told by security someone would be out to get me soon. Right around noon a female officer came and escorted me to a small bathroom and patted me down. That is right, a female officer. Upon conclusion, she told me I had one minute to say goodbye. I kissed my sister, shook hands with Ronnie, and then hugged and kissed Felicia. She was quite broken up. I tried to keep it together. They turned and left and as I was escorted down a hallway, I looked back and suddenly felt hopelessly alone. After being fingerprinted, mugshot, and strip-searched by a male this time, I was handed prison khakis, and taken to a dormitory that housed about fifty-five to sixty inmates.

I was led to my bunk (a top bunk) unloaded my stuff into my locker and headed to the dining area for lunch. my prison term had officially begun.

Later that evening, I made a monumental error: Every day at the hours of 4:00 pm and 9:00 pm, midnight, and 3:00 am, an entire headcount of the facility is taken. Ironically, it is called a stand-up count, can you believe it a (STAND UP) count which meant everyone out of bed and standing at the foot of their bunk. Also, during the count, no one under any circumstances is to leave their room (or in my case dormitory) until the count is cleared, which means everyone is accounted for.

So, it was the 9:00 pm count and I was standing by my bunk when I suddenly realized I had to get to Hospital by 9:30 to get treatment, which at the time was Tagamet, for heartburn relief. In my haste, I rushed out of the dorm without being aware that the count hadn't cleared. On my way to the hospital, I began noticing I was the only one in the corridors. As I continued walking, I became aware that other inmates were just standing by their beds. They were looking at me like I was visiting from another planet. I now got the feeling that something wasn't quite right.

Suddenly, three officers at the end of a hallway were yelling at me. Now I was sure I screwed up. They asked where I was going, and I said, "to the hospital". They then asked, "Do you know that count hasn't cleared yet?" And I said, "No, sir." Then they asked how long I had been here, and I said, "I came in today, sir." One officer said, "I'll take him back."

When we got to the dorm, the officer screamed at the inmates. "Did anyone tell him count hadn't been cleared?" To a man, they said they never saw me leave. The reason this is a big deal is that if you screw up the count, you are given an incident report– or in prison lingo a "shot". Getting a shot can result in a loss of good time or even a week or two in the County Jail. Luckily, I dodged a bullet.

Next day: Up at 6:00 am, off to the prison hospital for a complete physical. First stop, dentist. Not really, he was another inmate who supposedly had some training in dentistry. Next, a quick chest X-ray. A two-minute visit with a psychologist, followed by a hearing test, blood pressure, ears, eyes, nose, and throat. And finally, a blood test. I assumed this guy was a doctor because he had a stethoscope.

Whoever he was, he couldn't not find my vein with a search warrant and a floodlight. My arm was black and blue for a week.

After dinner, I moseyed down to the baseball field. I learned they had softball teams and I asked how I could get on a team. I played softball for years, so I felt good about playing and thinking it might feel a little bit like home. Great news, I tried out at third base and left field and made the softball team. It was the first time since arriving that I felt a little bit excited.

The weekend has arrived. I am trying to find things to keep me busy. The weather was rainy and chilly, so I headed to the gym for a while, then off to the library and the TV room. There is a movie on HBO I've seen several times, so I head to my dorm. Lying on my bunk, I am thinking it's the weekend; I should be performing at a comedy club. Instead, I'm incarcerated in rural Pennsylvania. Regardless of my situation, I must try to stay focused on my career. For the first few days I was involved with the softball team, working out in the gym, reading in the library which has taken up a lot of my time. But now It's Monday morning and I'm off to orientation for a two-day session and upon completion, I would be assigned a job. There wasn't any particular job I was interested in, but I was asked to submit an inmate request form—or in prison lingo, a "cop-out". I didn't care what job I got, I thought I'd just let the chips fall where they may. On the evening of the last day of orientation, I checked the bulletin board.

I was assigned to the electric shop. ELECTRIC SHOP? All I know about electricity is you flip a switch and the light goes on. Up to that point, my crowning achievement in electricity had been screwing in light bulbs.

On the first day of work, I met my foreman, a grizzled old coot who was very adept at insults. He also was anti-establishment and would watch his workers backs as best he could, plus work wise he would go easy on his inmates. So, it was a tradeoff: for the protection and light work, you had to endure verbal abuse. He also has nicknames for everyone. Mine was "Eek with a beak, is that your nose or a hose?" I thought I would deal with the nonsense to get my extra good time, which would help reduce my sentence.

There were two phone banks in the institution for the inmates to use. They're equipped for collect calls only. Five phones on the south wing and five phones on the north wing.

There was a sign-up system: you sign your name and when a phone becomes available, you write down the number of the phone 1 through 5 on the south wing and 6 through 10 on the north wing. The caller is allotted ten minutes; and all calls are recorded. If you go over your time you could be hit with an incident report, i.e. a "shot". The phone hours were Monday through Friday from 6:30 am to 7:30 am and 4:30 pm until 11:55 pm.

After making a call to Felicia around 9:00 pm I decided to walk around the facility, I spotted a chapel. I also noticed there was a Catholic Service at 9:30 pm. I had not been to church in a long time due mainly to the hypocritical stuff you see at a typical Sunday mass. But I thought under these conditions I would give it a try.

The priest was a pleasant man with a good sense of humor. He was from the local parish and although his service was done formally, after service he would talk to us in layman's terms. The informal talk was very personable, and I enjoyed it very much. For the first time in a long time, I felt spiritual. In just that one night, I gained an entirely different outlook and motivation to be the best person I could be for the duration of my time here.

I began a routine of watching inspirational videos. I also became a regular attendee at Catholic services and even joined the choir. I am not a singer but that didn't matter much. It was the spirit that counted.

I was not happy working in the electric shop. I wanted to get a different job. When I was not working, I would spend time in the library, and thought that would be an ideal place to work. I could study, I could read and most of all it would be a great place to focus on writing new comedy material. I started asking other inmates who were working there on how I could get an opportunity when a position became available. I was told to take it up with my counselor.

As an electrician's assistant my job was boring which made the time pass slowly. It consisted of carrying ladders, replacing light bulbs and handing tools to the electrician. As boring as it was to me, my real job was to stay focused on restarting my career. I just received my scores on my basic education test. It was a total of five subjects with 8 being a passing grade and 13 would be a perfect score. My scores were: spelling 13, English 13, literature 13, social studies 13, and math—which I considered my strongest subject— 9.7. I got a little tripped up on algebra, which I never used in real life, just what I recalled from school.

More and more I became passionate to secure a position in the education department. I figured it would be a positive environment where I could stay focused on my goals. I was determined to make it happen. I went ahead and filled out an Inmate Request form for any available position in the education department. They reviewed my request and based on my scores I was granted an interview for the position as a teacher's aide. It consisted of tutoring other inmates and a little orderly work. To secure the position, I needed a G.E.D. The test was only 8th-grade level, but 85% of the inmates flunk the language portion. Remember, I got a perfect score on that portion,. So, based on my scores I was set up for a G.E.D. test. I completed the test and headed to the library. My G.E.D. teacher stopped by the library to give me my scores. A perfect score was 27. My score was 24, and she seemed overly impressed. Within a couple of days, I got the news that I was hired. Now that I passed my G.E.D. test with flying colors, I finished my last day in the electric shop and prepared myself for my first day on the job. My days are now becoming full: tutoring inmates, doing orderly work in the library, softball games, writing new material, spending time in the chapel, waiting to make phone calls to my booking agents, and Felicia. My head is in a good place now, knowing that each passing day gets me one step closer to my dream. Make no mistake, losing your freedom is an amazingly difficult adjustment. The simple daily pleasures I enjoyed were taken away. It is hard to imagine until you've lived it. I am learning a tremendous lesson being here. Aside from the poor judgment and bad choices I made that got me here, and for which I am deeply sorry, I have learned how devastating losing your freedom can be. If you are not careful, your mind can play tricks on you. Sometimes in a moment of weakness, I think about not being able to make it back. What if I have lost it? What if

I am not funny anymore? I must stay positive. I quickly snap out of it and reflect on the accomplishments I've amassed in my career in a relatively short time and I gain the reserve to know I will come back and be better than I ever was before. It's been a couple of weeks and I'm enjoying my new job; it's rewarding teaching some of the inmates. Most of them want to learn although some of them are there just to kill time. After tutoring, I sweep, mop, buff, and dust. After my work day is done, I spend a lot of time reading and writing. I'm focused on my first show back when the time comes. Today I looked in my mailbox and found something I have been waiting for: a computer printout of my sentence and projected release date, which would be June 26th, 1990. However, I'm entitled to statutory good time, which makes my release date April 1st, 1990. It seems like poetic justice that my release date would be on April Fool's Day. I have finally been moved from the dormitory into a four-man room. There's word out that there may be a librarian position opening soon. I will make every possible effort to pin down that spot. I pick up my daily mail, letters from Felicia, my Mom, my sister Anne, and several comics. Because of the business he was in, my brother "Duke" was told by his boss not to contact me. It was hard to deal with even though I was told that would be the case once I was sentenced. I continue to keep busy, and it seems like I can see a flicker of light at the end of the tunnel. I continue to work relentlessly on my comedy material. There is so much humor here. I know that sounds ridiculous, but I am looking at it from a comedian's point of view. Right from the beginning, things that have taken place here are so hysterical and the comedy resources seem inexhaustible. I found myself consistently using the word "idiot" so I starting writing down stupid things people would do and say and finally it hit me. That will be the essence of my stand up, and my mantra will be "We're All Idiots."

Chapter 14

I have been writing a brand-new act based on that premise. No more prop bag. No more wigs. No more curlers. From now on it will be straight standup comedy for me. I have a meeting coming up in a couple of days with the educational supervisor to discuss the librarian's job. Things are looking up as I was just informed that I've been moved from a four-man room to a two-man room. By the way, the food here is not of the five-star caliber. For example, this morning for breakfast, the menu was pancakes and sausage. The pancake was like a discus; the sausage patty was like a hockey puck and the syrup tasted like transmission fluid. I went with a box of cheerios. After weeks of doing a superlative job as tutor and custodian I was rewarded with a position of library clerk. My new job is to keep shelves clean, neat and tidy, handle all the books being taken out or taken in, as well as assorting the weekly delivery of newspapers and magazines. My pay, a whopping 11 cents per hour. On a social level I am proud to announce that our softball team just swept a double-header and became the institution champions. I had two great games, getting nine hits in eleven at-bats. It was a great feeling. On the work front I just got my first job evaluation sheet. It is based on a one to five scale, five being outstanding. I received fives in all categories. For my outstanding work, I received a generous $6 bonus. Time continues to pass, and I get another step closer to renewing my dream. It's been a few months now, and I know it will eventually end and I can restart my life, my dream, my career. After work, I head to my unit and I'm stopped by my counselor who tells me he must deny Barry Katz's visit request. He shows me a printout from the crime commission and notes two various felonies. As I examine the document, I notice it states that the subject was 5'7" and weighed

135lbs, brown hair, brown eyes, and born in Louisiana. Barry Katz is 6'2", 220lbs, light hair, light eyes, and born in Massachusetts. Eventually, it got straightened out and Barry was awarded visitation. As I move forward in this journey I realize how a lapse of good judgement can be life changing. Prison is certainly a colossal reality check. I am certainly not alone in this venture. There are all sorts of professional people here who made poor decisions. Some men had huge businesses, there are doctors, lawyers, judges, politicians, as well as high ranking underworld figures all here doing minimal work, kitchen help, custodians, laborers, etc. It's been a long hot summer and as we begin the autumn season I'm still focused on my release, yearning to get back to my life, my career. I just had a nice visit from Barry Katz. That was the only time he made the 10-hour drive, but I appreciated it and was extremely excited to see him and talk "shop". I also got a visit from my girlfriend Felicia. It was a heartwarming visit and we enjoyed our time together very much. I must applaud the effort of Felicia by making that arduous trek every weekend for the entire duration of my stay. She was remarkable. The holidays were something special for me. Felicia sacrificed most of her time with her family during the holidays as we spent Thanksgiving and Christmas together. The dedication she showed throughout my incarceration left me in awe. Her love and devotion is something I will never forget. As 1990 rolled around I realized I'm getting close to my release date. It's been an astonishing odyssey to this point and a life-altering experience. I regret what I did to get here and I'm sorry for any pain I have caused, but I can assure you I will leave here a better person than when I came in. And now it's time to move on with my career, and my life. As my release date was getting closer, I was extremely excited and inspired. So much so that I went to my counselor and asked for approval for a stand-up comedy class. Several days later my requested was granted. It would be a 90-minute class, two days a week for six weeks, culminating with a comedy show in the gym. I stated on the message board that the top six in the class would perform in the show. The class attracted 15 inmates. I taught them how to construct a joke, material selection, stage presence, timing, etc. It was an awesome experience and a tough decision, but at the end of the semester, I made my 6 picks. The institution went all out for the event. The staff transformed the gym into a comedy club complete with checkered tablecloths, and candles on the table. The construction crew painted a sheet of plywood to resemble a brick wall backdrop. We even had a spotlight. I opened the show with 15 minutes of stand up and then introduced the acts, each performer allotted 7-10 minutes. The gym was packed, and the crowd roared with laughter. It was an unbelievable night. Later, the institution declared my comedy show was the best evening of entertainment in Its history.

I have been mentioning Felicia. Let me explain. I met her at Periwinkles in 1987. I hosted my show there every Thursday night called Ed Regine's Comedy All-Stars. One night, approximately a year after my divorce, I noticed a young lady sitting at the bar during my show. I went to the bar while a comic was on stage and started a conversation. After several minutes of chit-chat, I mentioned that after my show I was going to the Pancake House, and would she like to meet me there. She said she would. The show was over, and we left in separate cars. After a 15-minute drive we arrived and settled into a booth. We talked for an hour or so and then exchanged phone numbers and departed. After several lengthy phone conversations, I asked her out on a date, and she accepted.

After a handful of dates, I thought it was time to tell her about my history. I made it clear that to pursue this relationship any further would not be in her best interest. I pointed out that she needed to meet someone younger (I was eighteen years her elder) with a clean slate to start a family with. I also made it clear that at my age (forty-two), I certainly didn't see any kids in my future. Her response was "no way, I care for you very much and I want to be there for you." I liked her very much and I didn't want to end it, but I felt it was best for both of us, so sadly, I broke it off.

A couple of weeks later I was doing a show in Weston, Massachusetts, and Felicia showed up. After my show, she said she wants to be with me no matter what happens. She promised me she would be there for me always. I relented and said thank you, and we kissed, and our relationship was back on. Felicia went above and beyond the call of duty during my incarceration. She would not go into work on Fridays so she could make that 10-hour drive and stay overnight which enabled her to be at the facility as soon as visiting hours opened. She took care of all my personal matters and aided me through all the legal encounters. Her unwavering support was nothing short of incredible. While we were going through this process, Felicia and I grew closer together and at some point, we fell in love and discussed marriage. I agreed, but with the caveat of no kids. Was I selfish? Perhaps. But at my age and my career, I didn't believe I could be the dad that my child would need. Felicia agreed to no children. So, thanks to the kindness and determined assistance of Felicia, I was able to weather the storm.

I was released in March of 1990. A security guard drove me to the local bus station and handed me a bus ticket. I began my journey back into society. Felicia was there to meet me when I got off the bus. Our romance continued and flourished, and I was back to work. I was home in Rhode Island and performing all over New England again, as well as Las Vegas and Atlantic City. My first show back was a college in New Hampshire that Barry Katz booked for me. I was to headline with a 45-minute set. My opening act was Louis C.K. Louis did a great 30-minute opening and the crowd loved him. I started my act and I knew rather quickly I was going to struggle to get to 45 minutes. The crowd was great and laughing at everything, but I was running out of material. After a 14-month layoff it was clear to me that I was rusty. I finished my show and it went really well, but I could only muster 32 minutes.

In 1991, Felicia moved in with me in my Rhode Island condo. We were happy with our lifestyle of me performing and auditioning, and her working career. Felicia always tried to attend my shows as much as possible. She was also a huge help in promoting my career. When 1992 rolled around, which was approximately one year after she moved in, the subject of marriage came up more frequently. One day it reached a fever pitch with Felicia threatening to move out if I wasn't willing to commit. We went back and forth on the issue until she started packing. She was especially important to me and I truly did love her, plus I felt so obligated to her for all she had done for me during my incarceration. I apologized and agreed that we should be married. We set the date for September 1992.

While I was "away", my sister Anne had arranged moving my mom into a retirement community and after my release; Felicia and I would visit her often. One day, I got a call from my oldest sister, Anne, telling me that my mom was in the hospital. I went to visit her and knowing my mom, she wasn't happy being here. She made fun of the doctors and didn't even pay attention to what was wrong with her. I spoke with them and they told me they wanted my mom's permission to do a battery of tests. I said I would talk to her. After speaking with my mom, I knew there was no way to convince her to do these procedures. My mom vehemently refused any treatment and just wanted to go home.

Unfortunately, at this stage of her life and without medical attention my mom would be incapable of living alone, so my sister Anne said my mom would stay with her. I agreed. After several weeks, my mom's condition slowly deteriorated and in April 1992, my mom passed away at the age of 85. A week before my mom passed, I got a call from Bill Blumenreich the owner of the Comedy Connection in Boston telling me I got a spot on the TV stand up show called "Showtime Comedy Club Network" on The Showtime Network. My scheduled appearance was only two days after my mom's funeral. I felt like I couldn't do it. I was grieving and it was too soon for me to go back to work. Family members got together and convinced me to do the show because that's what mom would have wanted. With a heavy heart, I did the show and it went great. That night personified the phrase "the show must go on."

Chapter 15

I kept working and auditioning in Boston and once a month or so I would head to New York City where I would perform at the Comic Strip, Dangerfield's, and The Boston Comedy Club in Greenwich Village. One night at The Comic Strip, I was on the show with Chris Rock, Dave Chappelle, and Wanda Sykes. It was awesome working with this young group of comics who would go on to have exceptional careers. Whenever I would do spots in New York, I'd always be working with many of the nationally known comics of today. Names like Louis CK, Jerry Seinfeld Ray Romano, Rita Rudner, among others. On another occasion I was on the list to do a ten-minute spot, at The Comic Strip located on 2nd avenue on the east side. The Comic Strip was the club that launched so many comics including Eddie Murphy and Chris Rock. It was a packed house and I couldn't wait to get on stage. I checked the list and I was scheduled to go on somewhere in the middle of the show, Finally, I was next up. Just before I'm ready to go on, the club manager who was also responsible for booking the shows approached me and said, "Dennis Miller just popped in and wants to do about ten minutes, then I'll bring you on."

I absolutely knew this was going to have a bad ending, and boy was I right!! Remember at this point in time, Dennis Miller was nationally known and extremely popular. He began with some material and then started talking to the audience. Ten minutes went by and he has shown no indication that he is about to wrap up. He keeps going and the crowd loves it. I'm thinking I have to follow this. Believe me this situation is every comic's nightmare. Finally, after—I kid you not—forty-five minutes he ended. As the host of the show goes on stage to take Dennis off, the crowd starts leaving like the building is on fire. The host did some announcements and there are now six people in the audience, and two of them don't understand English. He then introduces me. Just five minutes ago, there was a great crowd laughing at everything, now it was a horror show. I bit the bullet and did my time.

I shared an apartment in the city on 82nd Street, between Amsterdam and Columbus. It was approximately 400 square feet and there were five of us. There was Barry Katz, Nick DePaolo, Louis CK, Anthony Clark, and me. The rent at the time was $1,000 a month, or $200 a month between us. We used it as a crash pad whenever we were in town, because at that point they were all still living in Boston, and I was in Rhode Island. Eventually, Louis CK and Nick DePaolo got their own apartments in New York. I made a career decision that I would leave as well and focus more on my career in New England. At that particular time Boston was a hotbed of comedy and Hollywood was shooting a lot of films there.

Not long after leaving New York, in September 1992, Felicia and I were married in the cathedral of Saints Peter and Paul in Providence, Rhode Island. We celebrated our honeymoon in the beautiful island of Aruba. Although Felicia's father didn't approve of us getting married, he was gracious during the wedding ceremony and also the reception. It wasn't long after that I seemed to have won him over and things were going well. The holidays came and went, and things were good.

1993 was an amazing year for me. I got more national TV exposure; I did shows such as Caroline's Comedy Hour, Comedy on the Road, as well as some local commercial work. I became the featured actor on many of the Rhode Island lottery commercials, also doing a commercial for the very first X-Games. Things couldn't get any better when I get a call from Felicia while I was performing in New Jersey that my ex-wife Carol has been shot.

I was shocked and immediately drove home to Rhode Island to be with my son, Ed Jr. My ex-wife was dating a retired Police Officer and during an argument, Carol (My Ex-wife) took out a gun. Folks, here's the crazy part: it was my gun. I had purchased it many years ago as protection, due to me carrying lots of cash when I was partners with my brother at the racetrack.

After the divorce from Carol, I went to the house for some belongings. I noticed the pistol was not where I kept it. I asked where it is, and she said she had thrown it away. I didn't think it was a good time to push the issue. I knew she was never pleased that I had it in the first place, so I honestly believed she did get rid of it. I simply asked how she got rid of it, and she said she threw it in Johnston Pond, which was not far from our house.

Once I got back to Rhode Island from New Jersey, I met my in-laws and my son. I gave my condolences to them and just wanted to make sure my son would be okay. The next day I got a call from the Johnston police department. They wanted to ask me a few questions. As you may know, in a situation like this the spouse becomes a person of interest. In this case, I was not as it was verified; I was in New Jersey at the time. It was when they showed me the gun that my heart sank. It was my 22-caliber pistol. I felt like if only I hadn't bought that gun so many years ago, she still might be alive today.

The detectives told me it was a domestic dispute and Carol had run into the bathroom with the gun and then her boyfriend heard a shot and broke the door down and rushed in and saw she had shot herself in the chest. I have never in my life ever heard of someone committing suicide by shooting themselves in the chest. The police were more than skeptical themselves but said that they couldn't find anything at the crime scene that would dispute the boyfriend's statement. However, as I am writing this, the case has just been reopened by a cold case investigator.

In June of 1993, I got a call from Bill Blumenreich the owner of the Comedy Connection in Boston. He asks me if I would be interested in opening for Andrew "Dice" Clay. Apparently, "Dice's" opening act had left him, and he was looking for a local comic to open for him on the weekend he was to appear at the Comedy Connection. Bill stated that "Dice" wanted someone who was Italian looking, was funny and had good energy on stage. Bill thought I would be perfect. I said, "I would do it" and he said, "I'll call you back with the official word".

When I hung up the phone I began pinching myself. Is this for real? Opening for Andrew "Dice" Clay? I was extremely excited and hopeful it would come to fruition.

The next day, Bill called me and said, "it's a go". There would be two shows on Friday and two shows on Saturday. What an amazing opportunity to meet and to perform with "Dice". I also felt that it could possibly enhance my career. On Friday I left my house early and drove the one hour or so trip to Boston. The shows were at 8:00 and 10:00p.m. I arrived around 7:00, parked my car and walked to the club. The Comedy

Connection was in an old building, one of several in an area known as Faneuil Hall. It was also located adjacent to the old North Church. The entire area was dripping with American History. I entered the club at approximately 7:30 and the room was filling up quickly and there also was a waiting line. I went to the dressing room to get settled. By now the room was filled to capacity which was approximately 500 people. At around 7:45, "Dice" along with his road manager, Johnny, had arrived and we exchanged pleasantries, I quickly realized that "Dice" was behaving exactly as I remember watching him on one of his HBO specials. I still wasn't sure at that time if he was just acting as his character or if this was who he really is.

In what seemed like a flash, it was showtime and the local host introduced me. I was scheduled for a 30-minute set and had no restrictions on my show's content, except the "C" word. Now, up to that point in my career, my act was considered PG but because of "Dice's" fans, I knew I had to up my act to an "R." I wasn't comfortable doing that type of an act, but I wanted to make sure I got the job done so that took precedent. I planned to do my edgier material and spice it up to Dice's crowd level.

I remember the audience was polite for a "Dice" crowd. As I found out later that was not usually the case. The Comedy Connection's crowd was great, and I had an awesome set. "Dice" went out and did his usual stuff and the crowd was eating it up. Back in the dressing room, "Dice" congratulated me on my show, and we chatted for a bit. I noticed that "Dice's" road manager, Johnny; appeared to like me and I felt a good connection with him. The second show, once again to a packed house, went great. I didn't stay for "Dice's" second show as I had to get back to Periwinkles in Providence to do a late show.

Saturday I once again headed to the Comedy Connection early. It was another full house for the first show, and it went very well. I wasn't surprised that "Dice" was filling the room, and although his vast popularity and the ability to sell out arenas were behind him, he still had a following of diehard fans.

What happened next really took me by surprise. Bill, the club owner, approached me after my second show set and said, "Dice" would like you to stick around and join us after the show." I said "certainly". Luckily, I had no late-night show anywhere. After "Dice" finished his second show, Bill decided we should go to Chinatown for a late dinner, which was within walking distance of the club. It was quite an eventful night. I'm sitting in Chinatown having dinner with the owner of a major comedy club and Andrew "Dice" Clay.

I recall the food was great, the conversation was awesome, and the laughs flowed like a fine wine. As I sat there I got the feeling that this is where I belong. The night unfolded just like I had envisioned many years ago. My dream was becoming a reality. To put an exclamation point on the evening, when it was time to leave, Johnny pulled me aside and said, "Dice" really liked you and your act. Here's my card, call me on Monday." I was pumped up like a Macy's Thanksgiving Day balloon. I took the card, thanked him, and said goodbye to "Dice", I also thanked Bill for the opportunity, and floated home.

Sunday seemed like such a long day. I had a local gig Sunday night, but all day I kept wondering what that phone call Monday would be like. As Monday morning rolled around I was anxious to call. However, I didn't want to seem too eager. Even though "Dice" lived in Hollywood, Johnny lived in New York because he really didn't care for the LA vibe and he just loved living in the City. Finally, in the late morning, New York time I just couldn't wait any longer. It was around 11:30 a.m. in N.Y. when I called him. We made small talk for a couple of minutes and then what he said next knocked me off my feet. He said "Dice" really liked you and wants you to open for him at the Greek Theatre in LA". "WOW"!!

Chapter 16

The Greek Theatre is an Amphitheatre located in Griffith Park, Los Angeles California. It has a seating capacity of approximately 6,000. This would be the most important show at this stage of my career.

Johnny said he would make flight arrangements and I would stay in "Dice's" guesthouse, which was in the back of "Dice's" home located in the Hollywood Hills. I immediately thanked him and told him I would see him in LA. I was on cloud eleven!

I couldn't resist spreading the news to all my friends who were mostly comics. Once I told them, the news blazed across the state. I was contacted by local media for interviews and local talk radio stations wanted me to come in and be on the air. Then the Providence Journal, the biggest newspaper in the state of Rhode Island sent a reporter to meet with me to do an article on how I got to open for" Dice" at the Greek Theatre.

The reporter who interviewed me ironically was a fan of my stand up. He would occasionally stop in and see my show at Periwinkles. He had also written articles while he was covering my trial and did a huge article upon my return from my incarceration.

The gig at the Greek Theatre was about a week away, so I just kept working and waiting to hear from Johnny. A couple of days later, Johnny had called and gave me my flight information. I was to arrive a day before the gig so I would have time to settle in. He wanted to arrange transportation from the airport, but I insisted on renting a car because I wanted to do some sightseeing. I rode around Hollywood; Downtown LA and I drove past the Greek Theater.

Eventually, I drove to "Dice's" house. It was an impressive home, but not the sprawling mansion of some celebrities. It had a pool in the back as well as the guesthouse. "Dice" met me in front of the house and led me back to the guest house. He said, "when you are settled come in the house". Once I put my stuff away I went to the house and "Dice" introduced me to his then-wife, Katrina. She was very pleasant and down to earth. Not your typical celebrity wife, more like one of the women in your neighborhood. 'Dice' decided to go to the gym; he was always going to the gym. He asked If I wanted to go, but I told him I wanted to relax after traveling all day. Johnny had arrived as well and was staying in the house with "Dice"

When he got back, we had a bite to eat and "Dice" decided we should go for a drive. So, "Dice", Johnny "Hot Tub" (that was his nickname), and I all got into Dice's new Trans Am and went cruising down Hollywood Boulevard. It was mind bending. My very first time in Los Angeles and here I am driving down Hollywood Boulevard with Andrew 'Dice" Clay. To make this even more surreal, Dice stopped at a huge candy store and bought bags of candy for all of us. Incidentally, I never found out how Johnny got his nickname, as "Dice" would slap a nickname on everyone in his circle.

The next day was the day of the show. I was to hit the stage at 7:00 and do 30 minutes. We got picked up at "Dice's" house by a limo at approximately 4:30 and headed out to the Greek Theatre. Rush hour traffic was heavy. When is it not in Los Angeles? We arrived at around 5:30ish and headed into the dressing room. With so much at stake I thought I should be nervous, but surprisingly, I wasn't. It was more of an exhilarating feeling. I felt self-confident and was eager to get on stage.

I was introduced and hit the stage running. I was full of energy and excitement and the crowd loved me.

I'm sure there were at least 5,000 people in attendance. It was exhilarating, incredible, amazing, and so much more.

As I walked off the stage, I thought: This is exactly where I should be. This is what has been inside me since I was a little kid and it is happening for real. WOO-HOO!! "Dice" went out and did his thing and the crowd gobbled it up. There was an after-show party in the Green Room, which held about forty people or so. "Dice" was introducing me to some LA industry people like Joel Silver, John Singleton, and that's when I said something that I knew later was stupid. "Dice," says, "I want you to meet Ron Jeremy." For those of you who don't know who that is, Ron Jeremy was the most famous porn star in the world appearing in over 2,200 films. I said, "Nice to meet you, Mr. Jeremy, I love your work." YIKES!!! I love your work is the most common thing you can say to an artist and believe me I'm not a porn junky by any means although I'm not a porn virgin either. So, I knew who Ron Jeremy was. I'm fairly certain that the standard "I love your work" didn't apply in this case. At some point during the meet and greet, Johnny "Hot Tub" pulled me aside and said, "Dice wants you to be his official opening act and I will let you know the information as we move forward, OK"? I calmly said "OK!" However, my insides were swirling like black clouds in a storm center. Through all that emotion and excitement, I became the official opening act for Andrew "Dice" Clay.

When I got back to Rhode Island, I spread the word to my comic friends and once again the media got a hold of it and there were more interviews and articles written about me. I had now become a local celebrity. But I felt I still had bigger fish to fry. I was with "Dice" from June 1993 to February 1995. We did over 150 shows together and it was quite an experience, to say the least. We toured all over the US and Canada. While we were in Ottawa, people were protesting outside the theatre. Things were changing as we moved through the '90s. It was no longer the 80's where a comic has free rein to say whatever they wanted. But, in the '90s things and subjects became politically incorrect. One of the highlights of the Canadian tour, was doing a show at a lounge called Lulu's, which at the time was the biggest nightclub in all of Canada.

Working with "Dice" I had the opportunity to meet a lot of amazing people: Roseanne Barr, Dustin Hoffman, Dan Aykroyd, Cathy Moriarty, who played Vicki La Motta in the movie Raging Bull, and Katey Sagal who at that time was starring in "Married with Children" just to name a few. Things were going great, but not so well at home. Some of Felicia's girlfriends and female family members had gotten pregnant and every time she would hear the news, she would have a total meltdown. We kept arguing about having a child and although I felt sympathy for her, I just couldn't give in. We had an agreement and we needed to stick to it.

"Dice" had set up a live Pay-Per-View comedy show in 1994 which he called "The Valentine's Day Massacre." It was to be shot at Sony Studios in NYC on Valentine's Day. Felicia, her best friend, Lydia, and I drove to NYC where Johnny had set up reservations at the Four Seasons. Lydia had been a huge "Dice" fan before I ever met her, so Felicia asked if it was alright to invite her and I said "yes." At the hotel, Felicia said her family was going to watch the show and if I could please not do my "Dice" opening show, which certainly carried a firm "R" rating. I thought it over for a while and finally agreed to do more of a PG version of my show. Now, keep in mind, there were four other comics beside me, and they were "R" rated comics. But still, I decided to grant Felicia's wishes. I spoke with "Dice" before the show about this and he said I should do my normal Dice show, which was a strong "R," but he left it up to me. To this day, I regret giving into Felicia's request.

The show started with "Dice" as the host and he opened with 30 minutes of typical "Dice" material. Then from there, he would introduce the acts. I was first on the list and I knew that this was Dice's crowd, and after a half-hour of his material I would have my work cut out for me even if I did my "R" rated version. While "Dice" was on stage, I kept wrestling with the idea of switching to my "R" rated set. Because doing a PG set after Dice had done thirty minutes of his stuff would be comedy suicide. But I promised, I didn't want to go back on my word. So, I did my PG show to a lukewarm response, and I often wonder how it would have gone had I done my "R" set. I guess I'll never know. But I do feel that it couldn't have gone any worse.

In 1994, I had the opportunity to do the TV show "Evening at the Improv." I was scheduled to tape the show two days after the huge Northridge Earthquake. I was still touring with "Dice" and we did some of the biggest theatres in the country, including Atlanta, Milwaukee, Memphis, among others. While performing in Memphis, Dice arranged a private tour of Elvis Presley's mansion Graceland. He was able to do this because he had done a movie with Priscilla Presley called "Ford Fairlane."

It was a great experience and a gigantic thrill to actually be in Elvis's home. Graceland and the rest of my tenure with "Dice" was certainly a wild ride.

As I have stated, working with Andrew "Dice" Clay was a great experience. However, in all honesty, he was not the most generous guy I ever met. His lack of generosity was reflected in my paychecks. I got paid less money working on a national stage in front of thousands of people than I got paid to do an obscure comedy club. But I accepted the meager payments in lieu of moving my career forward,

Even though, I do believe I should have been rewarded for my solid shows and professional work ethic, but instead things were getting worse. The last nail in the coffin happened while we were performing at Rascal's Comedy Club in New Jersey. The deal was "Dice" would take the door and the owner would get all the food and drink. The room held approximately 500 people and the tickets were around $40-$50 and had a cash only rule. If you do the math, that's $20,000-$25,000 cash per show in Dice's pocket.

After the show on Saturday night, Dice talked to his wife and she said some outlet at his house had caught fire and she was concerned. "Dice" immediately canceled Sunday's show which was already sold out and he said he was taking the first flight out in the morning. I thought it was an overreaction, but what could I say? All through the time I worked with 'Dice', I was never paid what an opening act for a national headliner would receive. I wasn't privy to know what he earned and frankly, it was none of my business. But in some cases, like Rascal's, I could do the math. Which in that scenario, my pay amounted to approximately 1%? I knew other comics who opened for "Dice" and I was told that he didn't pay much money to his openers. But I was OK with that because I was earning on my own. When I was on the road with "Dice", it wasn't so much about the money as it was a career opportunity.

The end came when we were back at the hotel that Saturday night. There was a knock on my door, and it was "Hot Tub" Johnny and he hands me a check. I open the envelope. I see that he hadn't paid me the full amount. He had left out Sundays payment. I guess because he canceled the show. I was taken aback because I thought I should get paid for the Sunday show. After all, it was canceled through no fault of my own. I guess "Dice" wanted to know how I felt about it because five minutes after I got the check, "Dice" knocked on my door and asked if everything was okay. I said "yes," and that was the last time I worked with Andrew "Dice" Clay. There were other situations during the time we worked together, but this was the one straw that broke the camel's back. To this day, I now and then bump into "Dice" at the Comedy Store in Hollywood and we exchange pleasantries. I certainly have no hard feelings. I chalk it up as part of my amazing journey. The rest of the year was back to doing clubs and auditioning in the Boston area.

Chapter 17

My marriage to Felicia was becoming a concern due to her constant lamenting about having a child. The holidays passed and we both were feeling the strain of our relationship due to her now being dead set on having a child, and the fact that I wasn't going to dishonor the agreement we had made.

1996 started well and I was able to book three full-length feature films. One was "Celtic Pride" which was partially shot in Boston at the Old Boston Garden. I was cast as a ticket taker at the turnstiles into the "Godden." The movie starred Dan Ackroyd and Daniel Stearns as devout Celtic fans who concoct a scheme to kidnap the star player of the Utah Jazz, which was played by Damon Wayans. One of the producers thought it would be a good idea if they had a comedian perform to the hundreds of extras in the stands while the crew worked on setting up some shots. It was a total disaster. Several other Boston comics had rolls in the movie, and we all agreed that it was one of the dumbest ideas ever.

The other movie I was cast in was a film shot in Rhode Island, titled "Code of Ethics" brilliantly directed by a young lady, Dawn Radican. The movie had a good cast and the star of the movie was Melissa Leo, who later went on to win an Oscar for her role in the movie "The Fighter". In this movie, I auditioned for the role of Melissa's father. But after giving a great audition, Dawn the director thought I was too young to be Melissa's father and instead she cast comedian Pat Cooper in that role. However, Dawn liked my audition so much that she said, "I want you in my movie," would you like to read for the part of a radio talk show host?" I said "yes" and after I read the part, I got the movie.

The third movie I did in '96 was a movie called "The Mouse". It was based on the life of boxer Bruce "Mouse" Strauss, who was the ultimate opponent. The "Mouse" would go into the city of the local boxing hero and basically, he was there to lose. I was cast as a boxing promoter who must talk the "Mouse" into fighting the local fighter. It was a fun movie to shoot as it featured many of the boxers of that era. There was Randall "Tex" Cobb, Ray "Boom Boom" Mancini, trainer Angelo Dundee, Vito Antuofermo, among others. The star of the movie was John Savage. You may remember him from his role in The *Deer Hunter*. He played the "Mouse". It also co-starred Rip Torn. As you recall, he played Agent Zed in *The Men in Black* movies. It was a wonderful experience working with such amazing people.

Two major life altering events occurred in 1996 besides making the movies. One was the erosion of my marriage and how I came to perform on cruise ships. First, Felicia was putting heavy pressure on me to get a sperm test to see if there was a reason she wasn't getting pregnant. I thought I would do it to calm things down for her sake. So, I reluctantly agreed just to ease some of the pressure. In the many discussions Felicia and I had about this, there were times when under relentless pressure, and because I cared for her, I left the door slightly ajar saying that maybe I would reconsider. I know in my heart that was wrong and I should not have given her false hope, but I did semi-crack under the onslaught of crying and fighting over this issue. The results of the test showed I had more than enough sperm, however, there were not good swimmers. So, the doctor said that it would take artificial insemination to achieve a pregnancy. We have reached the crossroads in our marriage.

The second major event occurred one night after my two headlining shows at the Comedy Connection. The manager/booker of the club Paul Barclay casually started a conversation with me and at one point asked if I had ever thought about performing on cruise ships. I said "never", and he asked why not. I answered, "that cruise performers were mocked as "Hacks" and it was somewhere that performers could work when they were unable to get work anywhere else." Some comics I knew were labeled with the derogatory title of "A cruise ship act". He said I don't mean this in a bad way, but I think your act would be perfect for a cruise ship venue. I felt a slight resentment, but at that time it was apparent that more comedy clubs were closing, and more comics were finding it difficult to get work. I was willing to listen. He mentioned that a couple of local comics, like Rich Ceisler, (remember him?) were performing on ships and doing well. He thought I should at least give it a try. He gave me the information of an agent in New York who specializes in booking comedians on cruise ships, and I should send her a tape of my act. I thanked him and told him I'd think about it. Late that summer after much consideration I thought what I have I got to lose, so I decided to send my tape to the New York agent. Several months had passed as I kept stalling for the artificial insemination procedure, I called the New York agent and she said she hadn't looked at my tape yet.

Shortly before the holidays, I convinced Felicia we would do the procedure after the holidays. She agreed and things at home settled down. It was early December that I thought I'd give it one last try with the New York agent and then move on. When I called, she answered and said, "I watched your tape and thought it was great, and we need to meet before the holidays." I agreed and we set up a meeting in NYC. Her office was on Long Island, so she took the train into the City and I drove from Rhode Island.

We met at a restaurant in Manhattan and exchanged pleasantries. Her name was Dee and Her agency was the "Dee-Mura" agency. We chatted for a while before getting down to business. She wanted me to sign a three-year contract with her as my manager and she said she would start booking me immediately on cruise ships. I liked her and her no-nonsense approach, so I agreed to sign with her. As we were leaving, she said, "You will hear from me right after the holidays." She was right on. In early January 1997, Dee called and offered me a two-week engagement on Royal Caribbean's brand-new ship, The Grandeur of the Seas. I thanked her but objected to being away from the comedy scene for two weeks. She tried to convince me that it would look good for future bookings if I accepted. I didn't want to do it but something inside me said "go for it". So, I accepted.

Back at home, Felicia was relentlessly applying the pressure again, so I said I would do it when I return from the two-weeks on the Grandeur. The booking was February 22nd through March 8th. As I left for the cruise, I knew I had two weeks to soul search and find out what my heart and mind would let me know the decision I needed to make. Mysteriously, on the very first day I left, I felt it in my heart that as much as I cared for Felicia, I couldn't go through with it. And I further believed, in the long run, it would be best for her. She would still be young enough to find love again and have the family she always wanted. Was that accurate or was I just being selfish? As it turned out, Felicia remarried not long after our breakup, and as far as I know, she has two children and is doing well. That makes me happy.

I landed in Fort Lauderdale on Friday afternoon and overnighted in a hotel there. I boarded the ship Saturday morning shortly after 11:00 A.M. I met with the cruise director that afternoon. He informed me that my first show was Thursday which meant I had 5 days before my show. I walked around to get my bearings, and to check out the showroom where I would be performing. It was an incredibly beautiful ship. Later that evening after dinner as I was walking around, I stopped into a lounge and noticed that there were only four people in there: a couple and two women sitting by themselves. We began introducing ourselves which led to small talk. After a relatively short time, the couple left, and I was there with the two ladies. We continued to chat for roughly half an hour when one of the ladies who was named Lexene decided to go to her cabin. Now it was just me and the other lady.

Her name was Debra and she was a hairstylist from Chicago. I must say from the very first moment I met her I felt something I've never felt before. I felt like I never wanted to stop talking to her. I felt compelled to be close to her, not in a sexual way but more of a spiritual manner. Because we were the only ones left in the club, I asked her if she would like to go for a stroll on the outer deck to enjoy the gentle Caribbean breeze. While I was walking around checking out the ship I had noticed a star gazing chart. I mentioned it to her and asked and if she would like to check it out. She was a bit skeptical, but she agreed. It was a warm balmy evening as the moonlight shone across the ocean. We stayed out on the deck watching the stars and talking for hours. I was captivated by her. She was warm, friendly, smart, funny, and loved life with a passion. Finally, at approximately 4:00 A.M. we decided to say goodnight. She said, "she would be out by the pool with her friends around lunch time so if I get a chance to stop by and say hello". Casually I said, "If I decide to go to the pool I'll stop by".

I went to my cabin that night, more accurately early that morning. I tried to sleep but I couldn't. I just kept thinking that my whole life has just been turned upside-down.

The next day I was walking on the pool deck for exercise when I noticed Debra and her friends. I got a twinge in my stomach when I saw her, but I played it cool as I stopped to say hello. The lady I met at the club Lexene and a married couple who were friends of Debra's Mom was there. She introduced me and we all made small talk for a few minutes and they invited me to have dinner with them and I graciously accepted. Although Debra and I talked for hours that first night, we didn't touch on anyone's personal life. Up to this point, I had only told her I was a comedian who was performing on the ship. I was churning inside wanting to tell Debra everything, but I wanted the time to be right. Debra had originally booked the cruise with her mom, but her mom had gotten sick just before the cruise. Debra wanted to cancel, but her mom insisted she go. So, Debra invited Lexene to take her Mom's place. After a wonderful dinner and great conversation, Debra and her friends had planned to go see the singers and dancers show and asked if I wanted to join them. I mentioned that I would love to, but I wanted to meet up with the production manager to discuss what I needed for my shows. They totally understood. Before we parted I asked Debra if she would like to meet me after the show for a drink. She agreed. We sat in a quiet lounge and I felt it was the right time to explain my situation. However, when I mentioned that, Debra insisted on telling me her story first. She started by telling me she owned a hair salon in Long Grove Illinois which is a suburb of Chicago. She said she had two daughters and had been divorced for eight years and had a male friend, but it wasn't serious. I began to tell her my situation and it was very emotional for me. She was incredibly supportive and although I felt like I was a horrible person for what I was going to do, she said I shouldn't blame myself. She was very comforting and understanding. She listened attentively to my every word. Again, we talked for hours and it seemed to be so easy and how time would pass so quickly. Debra and I spent so much time together that entire cruise and then suddenly it was over. The morning of her departure we met for breakfast and exchanged phone numbers. She said, "If you need to talk, call me" and we said goodbye. After she left, I had this empty feeling like I had lost something. My heart was telling me I must see her again. But part of me was feeling terrible about what was to happen when I got home. The next week on that ship was one of the most difficult times of my life. When I returned home, I sat Felicia down and told her I just couldn't go ahead with the procedure. She became hysterical and pleaded with me to reconsider. I felt like the most horrible person on the planet. I tried to explain that it is the best for both of us, but to no avail. Whatever love she had for me had quickly turned to hatred. After five years of a bitter sweet marriage, we were divorced in 1997. I was feeling like a heel, so much so that in the divorce proceedings I gave Felicia my condo and everything in it as well as the bank account we had shared. I left with just my clothing. I had called Debra several times just to have someone to talk to. 1997 was also the year my brother passed away due to lung cancer at 54 years of age. I was dealing with my brother's illness, my situation with Felicia, and talking to a woman I can't get out of my mind, all this and still going out on stage and making people laugh. As I think back I wonder how I was able to do it. At one point during the divorce proceedings, Debra asked if I would think about coming to Chicago for a few days just to get away from the hospital visits and the divorce proceedings. I thought it would be a good idea. It was nice to get away and I got to meet more of Debra's friends, her two daughters, her brother Dale, and her mom. When I left Chicago, I knew in my heart I was falling in love with Debra. On the day in court where we would be officially divorced, Debra insisted on being there for me. She flew into Rhode Island to lend moral support. It was an extremely emotional experience. When all was said and done I left the courtroom officially divorced. It was a very difficult day for me. I was so glad Debra was there. It didn't take long after that day that Debra and I had fallen madly in love with each other. Based on the events leading up to our meeting, we felt that we were soul mates and that our relationship was meant to be. We had reached a point where it was imperative to be together. I thought it would be a good idea and wouldn't hurt my career if I moved to Chicago. Debra thought differently. She said my entire stand up and acting career was basically in New England and she could use a change, so she insisted she move along with her youngest daughter, Shawna, to Rhode Island. Her older daughter, Stacy, had always been a rebel and because she had a boyfriend, she decided to stay in Chicago. We tried to convince her to come with us, but she refused and because she was over 18, she was an adult who could make her own decisions. Shawna was 15 at the time and basically had no choice. Although she was upset about moving, she settled in nicely and to this day she considers Rhode Island her home and me as her dad. So, the decision was made. Debra found a buyer for her salon in Chicago and I was saving money and together, we bought a townhouse in Warwick, Rhode Island.

Chapter 18

I was doing quite well working on cruise ships, land gigs, and acting so Debra officially retired. She began traveling with me on ships and she absolutely loved it. She had started a new life and she was thrilled. We were incredibly happy, and Shawna was doing wonderfully. We began planning our wedding and we decided we would do it while on a cruise ship. We registered to be married on the U.S. Virgin Island of St. Thomas. On August 5, 1998, Debra and I were married at Bluebeard's Castle overlooking the beautiful harbor of St. Thomas. Dale (Debra's brother) was my best man and Sheila, Debra's best friend was the maid of honor. Shawna and Ed Jr. were there as well. We all went back to the ship after the ceremony and had the reception dinner. It was a spectacular day and night. Things were going great, Shawna has settled into high school, Debra had made friends and we both were traveling all over the world. In 1998, I did my second movie that year, called *Next Stop Wonderland*. It starred Hope Davis, and in a small role, Phillip Seymour Hoffman. Hope Davis' character and Phillip Seymour Hoffman's character had broken up from their relationship and Hope Davis's mom in the movie signed her up for a dating service. I was cast as one of the responses from hell. It was a fun shoot, and what started as an independent film got picked up by Miramax Studios. Also, in '98, Dee had offered me a cruise to the Far East aboard Crystal Cruise Line's ship called the Symphony. I thought this might be a once in a lifetime opportunity. Cruising the Far East on a 6-star cruise ship. Although many entertainers are booked all over the world, for me as a comedian my locations were limited due to the language barriers. Regardless, I immediately accepted. I requested Debra to be my guest and the cruise line granted it. The itinerary was to fly to Hong Kong, overnight there, board the ship the next day, and sail to several ports including Vietnam, Thailand, Malaysia, and get off the ship in Singapore, overnight there and fly home the next day. The booking was 12 days for us, as it was a 140-day cruise around the world. It was an amazing experience and one I'll never forget. 1999 was another great year, Debra and I kept traveling, I was headlining all over New England and also had become the top reporter for a Rhode Island cable network called City Life Productions. I was also doing "On the Scene" reports including first hand reporting on the mayor of Providence, Vincent "Buddy" Cianci. I covered all major events in Rhode Island. I hosted auto shows, home and garden shows, and more, all at the Providence Civic Center. I also did sports commentary for championship boxing, and high school super bowls, plus, on location for newsworthy events. I had a full plate, but I felt I was ready to take on Hollywood. Debra and I talked about it many times and finally, she put her foot down and said when Shawna graduates from high school in the spring of 2000, we are moving to Los Angeles. I asked her if she was sure and she said, "I've never been more certain in entire my life". That was enough for me! While Shawna was still in school, Debra and I took a trip to Los Angeles to scout out some areas where we might like to live. After looking at various places, we decided to settle in the San Fernando Valley. We sold the townhome in Rhode Island, furnishings and all. We left with nothing but the clothes on our back and a dream. Along with our new high school graduate Shawna, Debra and I were on our way to the glitz and glamour of Hollywood.

In September of 2000, we officially moved to Los Angeles to further my film and television career. Debra and I bought a condo in the San Fernando Valley in a town called Tarzana. In 1919 Edgar Rice Burroughs bought a tract of land in the San Fernando Valley and named it Tarzana after Tarzan the character he created. I leaned toward the Valley because I became somewhat familiar with it while working with "Dice". I explained it to Debra, and she was fine with it. My immediate goals were to get an agent and to schmooze the comedy clubs, especially the three major clubs: The Comedy Store, The Laugh Factory, and The Improv. I interviewed with many different agents, and I was also submitting myself through Backstage, an industry paper, but I really couldn't find the right fit for the first several months. One day in early 2001 I heard that the Friars Club in Beverly Hills was seeking younger members and were offering special deals to join. The dues would be minimal if you agreed to put together a show for Friar members and their guests. I thought this would be a great way to be seen by some industry people. I applied to Irwin Schaeffer the President of the Friars Club and was quickly approved for membership. I immediately started to put a comedy show together. I booked a lineup of other comics I knew and in front of a packed house we did the show and it went great. While a member, I met some of the legends of comedy who would frequent the club. I had the great honor of meeting Sid Caesar. At the time, Sid was a frail older man approaching 80 years old but was still very gracious. One day when I left the Friars Club and was driving down Santa Monica Boulevard. I approached a red light and pulled alongside a 1980's Cadillac El Dorado and sitting behind the wheel was Sid Caesar. And as I sat there, I wondered how many people who might have been in the same position as I was and yet would have no clue they were right next to a show business icon. I also had the extreme pleasure of meeting Milton Berle, who was a founding member of the Friars in 1947. I was fortunate enough to chat with him for a few moments. During our conversation, I somehow had mentioned I collected wrist watches. He told me he had a bunch of old watches that didn't work and if I'd like, he'd bring one in to show me. I jumped at it and said, "That would be amazing". Sure enough, several days later, I was having lunch at the club and Milton Berle walks in and before he sat down he came over and handed me an old watch. Much to my shock, he said "if you fix it, you can keep it." I still have that watch to this day, and I wouldn't sell it for the world. After I did my comedy show, the club entertainment director, Eric Streit, approached me and asked if I would like to open for Billy Crystal. Of course, I said "Yes". The show consisted of me opening for twenty minutes then Billy for thirty minutes and finally Billy's brother Richard who did a Frank Sinatra tribute would close the show. After the show, I chatted with Billy for a few minutes and he was gracious and told me I was "very funny." However, I must say Billy Crystal was not the high energy guy you saw on TV or in his movies, in fact he was somewhat placid. Regardless it was a huge thrill to spend an evening with him. Being a member of the Friars and meeting the old guard of comedy brought back many childhood memories of watching these men on a black and a white Television. The feeling I got meeting these comedy greats was truly indescribable. I can honestly say I don't think anything in my career now or in the future could ever compare with the time I spent at The Friars Club in Beverly Hills. Sadly, it closed in 2007 and in 2011 that beautifully designed building was demolished. The night of the Billy Crystal show I also met David Paymer who played Billy's brother in the movie Mr. Saturday Night which David was nominated for an academy award as best supporting actor in that film. As we chatted he said something to me that was a resounding wake up call. He said and I quote "You should be working all the time" unquote. He was right. I had to face the reality that I cannot travel the road to do comedy and cruise ships because I would rarely be in LA long enough to pursue film and TV. The time frame of booking an acting gig starts with an audition, several days later, a callback, and then perhaps several days after that, the shooting date. The entire process could take up to 2-3 weeks. So, unless you are in LA 24/7, it becomes a matter of being lucky enough to be in town for that time span. It became essential for me to find an agent that would be willing to work with me knowing my schedule. One lady agreed to represent me if I would give up comedy and do telemarketing to make myself more available for auditions.

I knew immediately when she said that she wasn't right for me. However, to try to make myself more appealing to agents, I decided to limit my standup to cruise ships, an occasional Las Vegas date or a major corporate event. No more weeks away from LA. It was time to end being a road comic. Finally, I had a meeting with an agent, Stuart Edwards from the Coralie Jr. Agency who understood what I was trying to do, and my game plan. He loved my body of work (Resumé) and we agreed to work together. I can tell you he was amazing, and we did some fantastic things together. Almost immediately he sent me out on auditions, and I started booking stuff. I booked a sketch comedy spot on the Conan O'Brien Show as well as the Jimmy Kimmel Show. I also started opening for many national acts. In 2005 Stuart got me an audition for a series of commercials. They were for "Borman Auto Plex", A group of car dealerships in Texas and New Mexico, owned by Frank (The Astronaut) Borman. I would be their spokesperson playing a character known as "The Car Fairy" However, there were no leotards or fairy dust, the character was a "Mob Boss" who would pay you a visit if you didn't take care of your car. I went in, nailed the audition and several days later I was booked to do the commercials. I did a total of 6 spots, which were shot on location in Las Cruces New Mexico. Things could not be going any better. In 2006, my wife and I were out for a drive when she saw this "For Sale" sign on a house in the city of West Hills, California. We made an appointment to look at it. It had an amazing view of the San Fernando Valley and my wife fell in love with it. We decided to put in an offer with the contingency of selling our condo. The offer was accepted, and we put our condo on the market. In less than two weeks we received an offer on the condo for more than our asking price. I was on a ship at the time and received a message from Debra that we had an offer from a musician. As I found out when I got home that musician was Russell Hitchcock, lead singer of Air Supply. In 2007, I got a call from my agent saying he set up and audition for me for the new Tom Hanks movie *Charlie Wilson's War*. I was on a ship at the time with Debra. We pulled into port in San Diego got off the ship and was having lunch in a local restaurant when I received the call. I explained that I was on a ship and couldn't make it. I don't know what I was thinking at the time because I didn't realize how important this was. Well, Stuart quickly gave me a reality check and scolded me that this was a Tom Hanks movie. I quickly got my senses back and told him I would be there. The audition was scheduled for the following day. As we went got back to the ship, I immediately contacted the Cruise Director and explained my situation. He mentioned something about a "Jones Act" and said he would see what he could do. A couple of hours later, he told me he cleared it so I could get off the ship the next morning in Catalina Island. Debra immediately called one of her best friends Barbara and asked her to pick me up in San Pedro. Of course, she agreed. Bright and early the next morning, I hopped in the shower, got ready and jumped on the first ferry out of Catalina Island to San Pedro. Debra and I discussed it and we decided that she would stay on the ship to finish out the cruise. The plan was for Barbara to take me home and I would jump in my car and drive to Paramount Studios. I knew I had ample time as my audition wasn't until 3:00. I met Barbara at 10:00 am and she dropped me off at home at approximately 11:30, I quickly jumped in my car and I was off. I arrived at Paramount around 1:00 P.M. I parked my car and walked to the cafeteria for lunch and also to study my sides. "The sides" is a term referring to the lines I would say in the audition. My role was that of a limo driver. I studied the sides as I ate my lunch. My role consisted of five lines. So, as I studied, I did some tweaks to the lines and a little improv. At 2:45, I entered the casting director's office and signed in. It's important to point out that the audition was being held on a Wednesday. At approximately 3:00 pm, I was called in. I entered a room and there was the Casting Director, Ellen Tracy, and a cameraman. She invited me to either sit or stand, I chose to stand. Then she told me to "slate." Slate means to look into the camera and say your name. I did and she said, "whenever you're ready." I took a moment to gather myself and began. I delivered the lines partially as written and partially as I improved them. When I finished, she said, "That was great?" Then, she said something that made my head spin. She asked, "Where are you this Friday?" I responded rather flippant and said, "Wherever you want me to be. She asked if I could be back on Friday at 2:00 pm. I said "absolutely". I called Debra and she was extremely excited. Friday morning at approximately 9:00 am I picked up Debra in San Pedro as the cruise ended. By the way, another important component to this story is that at the time I got the call from my agent, I had already completed all my shows on the ship. I believe that helped a great deal in allowing me to get off the ship early. Had I still had a show to do, it might have had a different outcome. We arrived at our home around 10:30. I helped with the luggage, took a shower, and got dressed for my callback. A callback means if, the director liked your taped audition you would be called back to be seen in person. Debra told me to break a leg, we kissed, and I was off to Paramount Studios. I arrived at approximately 1:30 pm and headed to the casting director's office. I signed in and noticed there were just me and one other guy waiting to be seen. I guess it came down to him and me. At 2:00 pm I got called in first. When I walked into the room, sitting there was the famous director, Mike Nichols. In a split second, my brain went into overdrive. My head was reeling as thoughts rapidly appeared of leaving school at 16, working in a stable, gambling with my brother, my years in the car business, my time incarcerated, the son of a taxi driver with no formal education, and years of frustration and tragedy. After all of that, I'm at Paramount Studios in the same room as Mike Nichols, and I'm here because he wanted to see me. It was more than overwhelming. I quickly refocused to the task at hand. Mike Nichols introduced himself and said thank you for coming and to start whenever I was ready. In the room with us were Casting Director Ellen Tracy and another man who was going to read the lines of the other actors who would be in my scene. I chose to do the improved version of the script. As I'm doing the lines, I notice Mike Nichols laughing out loud at some of my lines. When I finished, he then asked me to read it again only this time stick to the script. I said 'okay' and read the lines as written in the script. When I finished, he said that was great and shook my hand and thanked me for coming in. I also thanked him for the opportunity and thanked Ellen and left. As I was leaving, I wished the other actor the best of luck. I left the meeting feeling good about it. I called Debra to tell her how it went and then I called Stuart my agent and told him I thought it went well. Now to try and put it out of my mind and enjoy the weekend with my family. Monday morning at approximately 11:00 am I got a call from Stuart to congratulate me because I got the role of the limousine driver in Tom Hanks's new movie *Charlie Wilson's War*, which also starred Julia Roberts and Philip Seymour Hoffman. I barely could find the words to thank Stuart as I was euphoric. Debra was so happy for me that she was close to tears. What a wonderful moment. Yes, my dream is coming true!!

Chapter 19

A few days later I received my call time to report to Paramount Studios for my first day of shooting. I reported to wardrobe and was fitted with a limo driver's outfit; cap included, and then headed off to make up. When I first arrived, I met the second A.D.—assistant director—who escorted me to my trailer. In the trailer next to me was actor Ned Beatty, a great character actor who was known for "Deliverance" and the "Superman" movies to name a few. We met and chatted for a while and I must say he was very warm and friendly. Once the wardrobe and makeup were done, the second A.D. escorted me to a Paramount Soundstage. Set up there was an older Cadillac limousine from the '80s, which had been cut into three pieces. I was waiting on the set when director Mike Nichols approached me and asked how I felt and thanked me for being here. The crew was working feverishly setting up the shot. Suddenly, out of the corner of my eye, I spotted Tom Hanks standing close by. Now, up until that point in time I had worked with dozens of celebrities but seeing Tom Hanks I must admit I was star struck. Several minutes later, Mike Nichols wanted a run-through, which means do the scene without the cameras on. Mike Nichols then introduced me to Tom Hanks, telling him I was playing the limousine driver. I said something like "nice to meet you, Mr. Hanks," to which he responded, "call me Tom." The scene was me driving Congressman Charlie Wilson (Tom Hanks) and another politician plus a couple of hookers to the airport to drop off Charlie. Here is a little inside Hollywood information: we never left the soundstage. The reason the limo was cut into three pieces was because of the camera placement. I was sitting behind the wheel with a camera mounted on the front of the car. In the middle section was a cameraman and in the rear section were the other actors, including Tom Hanks. Now came time to roll cameras. Mike Nichols called "-action" and we ran the scene. We did several takes, mostly due to lighting, sound and camera placement. The process of shooting this one scene was enormous. It took the entire day. The Hollywood magic was the fact that we never moved, the limo never started up, nothing about the limo was real, as it had been gutted. It was just a Hollywood prop. If you have seen the movie or will see it, note that the driving sequence was all done with a green screen, which is a brightly colored neon green screen where images can be added to make it appear to be real action. So, my first day on the set was a success. It was on Monday and I was contracted for five days. I must tell you during downtime when the crew was resetting the shot, I would make small talk with Tom Hanks. I was amazed at how friendly and easy-going he was. He is the kind of guy you would love as your next-door neighbor. Day two rolled around and the shooting schedule had me driving into the Las Vegas airport to drop off Charlie. More movie trickery, the shoot would actually took place at the Ontario Airport in Ontario, California.

I had arrived early and was at Craft Services (which is an area with various snacks and soft drinks available) when I noticed a black Toyota Prius pulled up and who got out none other than Tom Hanks. I was extremely impressed that someone of his stature and star quality would not be chauffeured to the location. That just further emphasized what a regular guy Tom Hanks is. A few minutes later we were called to the set. We arrived and I quickly jumped into the limo which was a 1984 Cadillac. My job was to drive it to a designated mark. To enhance the scene, scores of vehicles from that time period were hired to drive around the airport as well. The crew had a boom camera mounted on a crane to capture the shot. In the limo with me was Tom Hanks, actor Brian Markinson, (you may remember him from the Robin Williams movie RV) and the ladies of the evening. Once I got familiar with the limo I realized it was not in great shape. The brakes were bad, and the steering was sloppy. I had made several attempts to hit the mark but failed. Let me also mention we had a crewmember in the car with a walkie-talkie so we would know when Mike Nichols would call "action". As I struggled to hit my mark, I began to get good-natured ribbing from Tom Hanks. On one retake, instead of circling the airport I decided to back up to my starting mark and accidentally hit a chain-link fence. That's when Tom Hanks said, "Ed, do you have a driver's license?" and at one point he jokingly asked me if he should drive. We all had a big laugh. Fortunately, before the day was over, I hit the mark, and everyone was happy. During one of my conversations with Tom, I expressed how much I loved his work and I specifically mentioned the film "Castaway" as one of my favorites. He was very engaging, telling me that the entire process of making that movie was a labor of love. At one point he asked me if I did anything else besides acting and I said, "I'm a standup comedian", he then asked where I perform, I said "I perform at corporate events, Las Vegas, Atlantic City, and a few of the top comedy clubs and luxury cruise liners". He graciously added, "Perhaps I'll see you perform on a cruise someday." I said, "that would be awesome", knowing that for all intents and purposes that would never happen. Several more days of shooting consisted of Tom getting out of the limo with the other actors and me retrieving Tom's luggage from the trunk. Also, as I bring it to him he hands me a tip says his goodbye and that was that. The next day we did some still shots and late Friday morning I was wrapped, meaning my portion of the filming was over. It was an amazing journey as I got to hang out with a great actor and a fine human being. It's something I'll never forget. As I write this, I continued to realize how incredible life can be. A stable hand with no formal education, rubbing elbows with some of the biggest names in show business. My dream is happening. In 2008, I got a call from my agent Stuart. He set up an audition for a feature film starring Barbara Hershey and Ron Perlman, and Co-Starring Daniel Gillies from the "Spiderman" movies. The role called for a lounge singer in a western bar and restaurant in Arizona. I attended the audition and there were lines, but I also improved using portions of material from my standup. The audition went well, and I left feeling good about it. Two days later, Stuart, my agent, informs me that I have a callback for the movie. I nailed the callback using some more improv and a several jokes from my act. I called my agent and told him I thought it went very well, and he said as soon as he hears something, he'd let me know. It wasn't long after that Stuart called and told me I got the part. The movie had an unusual title. It was originally called "Vacuuming the Cat" because in the movie Barbara Hershey's character would actually vacuum her cat. However, cooler heads prevailed, and the movie was retitled "Uncross the Stars." My agent informed me that there would be a table read, which means most of the actors would sit around a table and read through the script. The table read was held in one of the executive producer's homes in Hollywood. I arrived early as usual and waited for the rest of the actors. Just then, Barbara Hershey walked in and she looked as beautiful as I had seen her in some of her movies. She was very congenial and friendly and engaging. Unfortunately, Ron Perlman couldn't make the table read so the director read his part. It was a fun read and a fun afternoon. The director Ron Golde explained the shoot would be on location in Indian Wells, Arizona. The shoot, or at least my portion of it, was scheduled for three days. On the first day on the set, I met Ron Perlman. A great guy, he was friendly and easy to work with, but overall was kind of quiet. I also met Irma P. Hall; a character actress mostly known for her co-starring role in the Tom Hanks movie "Lady Killers." Irma and I discussed Tom Hanks and we both agreed he was an awesome guy. My acting career was flourishing, and my standup was still going strong, performing on cruise ships as well as cities like Reno, Las Vegas, Atlantic City. My plate was not only full, it was overflowing.

Chapter 20

Barry Katz had moved to LA in 1995 and suggested I should also move there. However, I elected to stay on the East Coast,. We really didn't communicate much until I finally moved to LA in 2000. Even after I moved there Barry and I only occasionally crossed paths as I was mostly at sea and busy with my acting career. Besides managing, Barry got involved in Producing. In 2004 I learned that Barry was producing a show called "Last Comic Standing." I called him and mentioned I'd like to do the show. He gave me the date of the LA auditions and taping. I told him I would be out to sea on a cruise ship and I couldn't break the contract. He asked, "where and when do you get off the ship"? I told him the date that I would be getting off the ship in Miami. He said, "the day after you get off, there are auditions at the Improv in Tampa, could you make it"? I told him I could. He said he would put my name in so when I got there, I wouldn't have to wait in line. I got off the ship, rented a car and began the four-hour drive from Miami to Tampa. I called my adorable aunt Angie who lives in Tampa and asked if I could spend a couple of days with her. Of course, she said "yes". When I arrived at my aunt's in Tampa she had dinner ready. We ate a delicious meal, chatted for a while and then I went to bed. The next day I showed up at the audition early as usual. Barry was not there, so I mentioned his name, and I was quickly escorted into the green room, a waiting room for performers, to get ready before going on. Finally, I'm called to go to the showroom. Sitting in front of me were several NBC executives. Keep in mind, there is no audience so there would be no laughter, just an eerie silence after every joke. I had two minutes to win them over. I went with my best stuff and at the end, Ross Mark and Bob Read, the talent coordinators form NBC, said: "that was great, we'll see you tonight." I passed the audition and was slated for a spot that night in front of a live audience to win the right to go to New York for the semi-finals. That night the Improv showroom was packed. As luck would have it, I was chosen to go on first, usually; a death kneel in any competition. The comics were allotted seven minutes. I went out and I say this honestly and truthfully, I had a killer set. I felt good about my chances as we were told NBC would pick two comics to advance to New York. I nervously watched all the other comics and I can tell you there was only one other comic whose set matched mine and that was an older female road warrior comic known as "Grandma Lee." The competition was over, and we were all called back on the stage. Bob Read, one of the executives, congratulated us on our performances and said, "although we were scheduled to pick two comics, we only have a slot for one." After the competition, I felt like it would be me and Grandma Lee, or at least one of us, but now with NBC only selecting one comic, things got a little stickier. Bob Read, the executive, said, "it was a very difficult choice, and after careful consideration, we are selecting Jim Norton." I stood there in shock. How could that happen? I was stunned. What came out later was that the second season, which I was in, was allegedly rigged. The judges in the finals, Brett Butler, Drew Carey, and Anthony Clarke all stated, "These are not the people we voted for." The backlash was so strong that NBC canceled the upcoming season of "Last Comic Standing." According to a March 2004 Pittsburg Post-Gazette article by Gene Collier, some of the comics in the opening rounds were plants hired by the producers to give bad performances on purpose to liven up the auditions on television. During season two in which I was involved, a panel of four celebrity judges was used to shrink the field of forty semi-finalists to ten finalists. The celebrity judges rated each of the semi-finalists as they performed and cast votes for the top ten comedians. When the finalists were announced, they didn't match up with the judges' votes. Two judges, Drew Carey and Brett Butler angrily got up from the judge's table and walked off. Carey called the show "crooked and dishonest." It was also revealed that some of the finalists were clients of the producers and directors of the show. That was season two, the season where I auditioned and killed.

Our first year in Los Angeles the three of us were doing what we could to get acclimated. Debra was making new friends, Shawna was enrolled in esthetician school and I was schmoozing at the comedy clubs, and of course, still performing on cruise ships and doing some acting. I got a call from a casting director who I had met on a previous audition and was asked to audition for a pilot for a new CBS version of "The Gong Show" hosted by Tom Arnold. I booked the spot and for my routine I would do the opening of the old TV show Superman backwards (spoonerism) and I did it in full costume. I was only supposed to do a little bit of it, but Tom Arnold was so mesmerized that I finished the whole bit. The panel of judges were Kathy Griffin, comedian Tommy Davidson, and actor Martin Mull. They were to judge my actions, but they were so taken by the bit that they were speechless. Tommy Davidson pretended to faint which I immediately took advantage of and ran over to him and began a mock version of mouth-to-mouth resuscitation. I was always quick on my feet. Unfortunately, the show never got picked up. One morning our phone rang—yes, we had a landline at the time—and it was around 5:30 am. It was my stepdaughter, Stacy, calling from Chicago telling us to put the TV on because some planes had just crashed into one of the World Trade Center buildings. I immediately thought it was an accident, however I turned on the TV and in shock and horror, I watched the second plane crash into the second tower. I couldn't believe what was happening. As the news and the pictures on TV emerged, I felt sadness. My heart was hurting watching what was going on. I also felt extremely angry toward whoever had done this. It was one of the most painful days of my life as Debra and I sat on our couch shedding our tears. Shortly after I arrived in LA in 2000 as part of my onslaught, I sent out videos, headshots and resumes to agents, casting directors, and all the late-night TV shows, not having any idea a catastrophic event was soon to happen. After the events of 9/11 Jay Leno, who took over the Tonight Show on May 25, 1992, started doing sketches about the terrorists. One day I got a call from Scott Atwell, the casting director for the Tonight Show. I assumed he had reviewed the promotional material I had sent to the show. Scott asked if I was available to do a sketch on the show. Of course, I said "yes". What a thrill this was for me. I checked in to the NBC studios in Burbank and because I arrived early as I usually do, before going to wardrobe I walked around the studio and then I stood on the stage of the Tonight Show where as a young boy I would watch the comedians perform on TV. I always dreamed of being there someday and here I am standing there and not on a tour, but as a guest of the show. Just the thought of it was overwhelming. I got to meet Jay Leno and he was, and is, a great guy. He thanked me for coming, welcomed me to the show and then went off to his office. I thanked him and went to my dressing room. I got into costume and went to makeup. I was exuberant. After makeup, I was called to the set. The sketch was two FBI agents dressed as limo drivers at the airport holding up a sign "Terrorist". I would walk off the plane, spot the sign and say, "yes, it's me" and they would immediately drag me off as I'm yelling "I am innocent". It was great. Scott called me the next day and thanked me and said the sketch was a big hit. Jay loved it, and Scott said he would have me back. I was super excited. Scott wasn't lying. Up until Jay left the show, I was a regular sketch comedy actor on the Tonight Show until Jay left in 2014. In total, I did over a dozen sketches and there would have been more but several times I would get a call from Scott Atwell only to be out of town doing my standup. The most popular sketch I did was playing the character Sanjay Leno, host of the Tonight Show in India. It was so popular that NBC put my character on the Tonight Show website. My time on the Tonight Show was truly an awesome experience. To this day I still hang out with Jay whenever I get the chance to see him at the Hermosa Beach Comedy and Magic Club. On any given Sunday night when Jay is in town he will do his stand-up show there. Another amazing opportunity came to me in the early 2000s. As I mentioned, I sent my promo out to casting directors, agents, and late-night shows. Well, one day I got a call from the casting director for Mad TV. There was no audition needed, Mad TV had seen my promo and I'm assuming clips from the Tonight Show, so they asked me to be a part of a sketch they were going to do. It would be a takeoff on the HBO show "The Sopranos." Of course, Once again I said "yes". The sketch was called "Where's the Gabagool," you know the Italian deli meat capicola. In the sketch, I was called into Tony Soprano's office at the Bada Bing strip club and beaten with a baseball bat for snitching on a "made man."

In the sketch, Tony reads me the riot act, I begin pleading and begging for my life, Tony finally is disgusted with me and instructs Big Pussy to shoot me. The joke in the sketch was that if the Sopranos were to appear on Network Television, what that would sound like. It was very funny because almost every other word you would hear a beep. It was an extremely popular sketch. So much so that HBO decided to put the sketch on the box set of "The Sopranos" and I am enormously proud to be a part of it. The years in LA were going great. Shawna had graduated from esthetician school; Debra had made a lot of wonderful friends. I was still traveling on ships with Debra and occasionally Shawna as well. Life in LA was wonderful. 2010 was another great year. I had done several short films and some commercials. I also traveled to New Orleans to entertain the new troops before there were sent to Afghanistan. It was such a rewarding feeling to give the young men some laughs before they are sent out to fight for America. These young men and women are truly my heroes. I toured with Fred Travalena and his lovely wife, Lois, and of course, Debra was there with me. I had met Fred Travalena on a cruise where he and I were booked on the same ship. This was in 1999. I introduced myself and told him I was a big fan of his even before I became a comedian. Fred was very gracious and from all indications seemed to be a genuinely nice guy. I met with Fred a couple of times for lunch while we were on the ship. At some point I mentioned I would be moving to LA soon. The day before we were to leave the ship Fred gave me his card and told me to look him up when I got settled in LA. I assumed it was just Fred being nice and I didn't think it would go anywhere. A month or so after we had adjusted to living in LA I was still schmoozing around. One day Debra asked, "have you called Fred Travalena?" I said, "no I haven't" She said "why don't you give him a call" I contemplated for a moment and then decided what the heck.

I called and got his secretary, so I immediately assumed I wouldn't hear from him. I was waiting for the usual "Fred is in a meeting and I'll have him call you back" and that would be the end of it. However, I was shocked when I heard Fred say, "Hello, Ed." I further explained who I was, and Fred said, "of course I remember you." We talked for a few minutes about where I was living and how was my move here and how am I doing. What came next really surprised me. He asked, "what are you doing this coming Saturday night". I said, "I have nothing planned", so he said, "I'll be attending a Las Vegas night at the Friars Club in Beverly Hills, would you and your wife like to join me and my wife Lois?" I said, "We'd love to". Fred said, "come to my house and we can all go together". I said "sounds great" I told Debra and she was excited to go. We arrived at the Travalena's and were invited in. The home was warm and decorated with many of Fred's accomplishments. Fred insisted we go in his car, Lois would drive, as I was unfamiliar with the area. When we entered the Friars Club, a funny thing happened. Debra noticed a guy standing nearby and said, "Do you see that guy over there? I know him from somewhere." It was so funny because the guy was Dick Van Patten from the hit TV show "Eight is Enough." There were many celebrities there and Fred graciously introduced us to them. It was the start of an amazing friendship. Fred and I became remarkably close, almost like brothers. We did shows together; we went out to dinner together. Lois and Debra also had also become close friends. In 2005, Debra and I attended the celebration of Fred getting his star on the Hollywood Walk of Fame, along with a host of celebrities who were also there to honor Fred. We had built a solid and never-ending friendship; we would have parties at each other's homes. Every Christmas Fred, and Lois would host a huge party at their home, and Debra and I would always be there. Fred, and I would perform in his living room and all the guests loved those shows, especially Fred's friend Wink Martindale, with whom I became friendly.

Fred Travalena was one of the greatest impressionists of all time and an amazing man. Sadly, Fred had gotten Hodgkin's Lymphoma and he fought it courageously, However, with deep sorrow, on June 28, 2009, Fred Travalena passed away at his home. It was a huge loss in my life. To this day I still miss him dearly. His loss left me with a heavy heart. Through it all Fred's wife Lois and I have remained close friends.

Chapter 21

Things were going extremely well, the travel was awesome, Debra loved our home and Shawna was doing great. She had gotten an amazing position at a beauty salon in Beverly Hills as an esthetician. While working there she met a hair stylist named Bulmaro "Bull" Garcia and after dating for several months they were married. To date they have blessed us with two wonderful grandchildren: Ava, 9 years old, and Gavin, who is 6. I continued auditioning and booking independent film projects and things couldn't have been any better, however there were dark ominous clouds ahead! Shortly after our marriage, I noticed that Debra would occasionally complain about stomach pains. She attributed it to Irritable Bowel Syndrome. This went on for many years and although she had regular medical check-ups, her Doctor agreed it was just IBS. As 2012 rolled around, she was complaining more and more about the pain in her stomach. I urged her to get another checkup, which she did and after several tests, doctors were still unable to find anything. Once again they concluded it was IBS. She was told to avoid food that she knew would upset her stomach. This went on for a many months, but even though Debra was watching her diet, the pain was getting worse. Finally, we scheduled a meeting with a Gastroenterologist specialist. During the meeting he suggested a more thorough test to see if he could pinpoint the problem. The test was scheduled for October of 2012, which would be as soon as we returned from a Bermuda cruise. That cruise was the crowning moment in our marriage. Every second we spent together was magic. that particular cruise cemented, without question that we were soulmates. Regretfully, that was the final cruise Debra and I would ever take together. We went to the hospital and Debra had the test. We had to wait a few days for the results. When the test results came in, we were devastated. The test showed a growth on Debra's pancreas. The doctor scheduled Debra for a biopsy. She had the biopsy and again we had to wait for the results. I remember we went to Santa Barbara for the weekend and walked along the beach. We had an amazing time soaking up the beach ambiance while just talking to each other. We shared some glorious and heart-warming memories. On Monday, the results of the biopsy came in and it was catastrophic. Debra's tumor on her pancreas was cancerous. We were absolutely crushed. Initially we cried until there were no more tears. But not long after our tears were spent, we swore to each other we would fight this with every fiber in our bodies. The odds were not in our favor which would only inspire us to fight harder. I immediately put my career on hold and dedicated myself to be with Debra every waking moment. We had scheduled a meeting with a surgeon who was going to perform what is known as a Whipple procedure to remove the tumor. But first, it had to be shrunken from 4 mil to 2 mil before Debra could have the surgery. This meant many rounds of chemotherapy. Together we endured the bi-weekly doses of chemo and after several months when her doctors decided she could take no more, they scheduled the surgery. At that point, the tumor had shrunk to 2½ mil. So, myself and my family felt somewhat hopeful and cautiously optimistic. However, the surgery did not go well. There were complications and Debra left the operating room in a coma. My brother-in-law Dale and my son Ed both flew out to California. Dale from New Mexico and my son Ed from Rhode Island. I was at Debra's bedside from 6:00 am until 7:00 pm every day 7 days a week and then Shawna would arrive from work and she Would stay until around midnight. Dale and Ed Jr. who were staying at our house would also come for a several hours each day. Debra stayed in the intensive care unit in a coma for eight days. It was so painful to watch her. A woman so active, so full of life just lying there unable to move. It was gut-wrenching. When Debra came out of it, we were all so happy and relieved. Now the long road to recovery had begun. The surgeon really could not say with certainty what happened in the operating room except that Debra had a serious bleeding issue. I'll never really know what happened, but in my heart, I felt it was a botched operation. To this day I regret I didn't pursue some sort of lawsuit to get to the bottom of it. But the grief was so overwhelming I could barely focus. My only objective was nursing Debra back to health. I know I could go on and on of how difficult it was for both Debra and me, but anyone who has gone through a similar situation would totally understand. Let me say that after hospital stays, rehab, and loving care, Debra for a few short weeks, was almost back to her old self. However, like an evil villain stabbing a dagger through our hearts, the cancer which stayed in check for a while was now was spreading. Eventually, Debra was hospitalized and never came home. On November 2, 2013, Debra, with me and our immediate family surrounding her, passed away in her sleep. I will say I suffered the excruciating pain of a broken heart, but I feel blessed to have known her and to have had a wonderful 16-year marriage. I hold in my heart and my head so many incredible memories that will stay with me for the rest of my life. I will never forget her and will continue to thank God for sending her to me. After things had settled down, I took several months off.

I stayed home for the holidays and organized a party in Debra's honor. It would be on January 6th Debra's birthday. I invited all her friends and of course our family. Everyone in attendance stood in front of a microphone and told their favorite Debra story. It was a great day and I'm sure Debra was looking down and laughing because one thing that Debra loved was having a party for friends and family. In the spring of 2014, approximately six months after losing my soulmate, I told my agents I felt ready to get back to work. They immediately started getting me cruise bookings and auditions. I booked some independent movies and did a couple of pilots while also doing some in concert standup performances. Things were getting back to somewhat normal. In December of 2014, fifteen months after Debra had passed, my agent booked me on a five-day cruise out of Tampa, Florida. The first night of the cruise was December 15, and I was scheduled to do my late night show at 10:00PM. One of my bits in my act was a spoof on the Miss America beauty pageant. I told the audience I was From New Jersey and explained why New Jersey doesn't always do well in the pageant and the reason was New Jersey doesn't always pick the right woman to represent them. After my show I was walking to my cabin and I get a tap on my shoulder. I turned around and it's a woman who says, "Where in New Jersey are you from?" Now I'm from Rhode Island, but I didn't want to explain, I said "Jersey City." She took issue with that. She said, "You're not from Jersey." She was definitely from New Jersey because she had that Jersey attitude. While this was going on, I noticed a lady was standing a few feet away. I didn't want to continue this conversation; I just wanted to get back to my cabin and chill out after my show. However, this lady wouldn't let it go. "Are you really from New Jersey?" I said "yes" and then she asked, "Where are you going," I said back to my cabin, she offered, "why don't you join us for a drink?" I said, "I don't drink", she said, "have a soda." She was relentless and hard to refuse so I agreed to go for a drink. She introduced me to her girlfriend; her name was Kristina. Ironically, the Jersey girl was named Christine, although spelled with a C instead of a K and lacking an A at the end. We sat in a lounge and chatted for perhaps an hour or so, and then they invited me to dinner the following night. I thought it would do some good if I got out and socialized a little, so I accepted. To set this up, I found out that Christine was married and Kristina had been single for eight years and had three kids, a son who was 22, two daughters, 18 and 15. When I met them in front of the dining room and saw Kristina that night, I got this butterfly feeling in my stomach and I knew that somehow Kristina and I had some kind of connection. From what information I had gathered I noticed there were coincidences between Kristina and Debra, they both had two daughters the same age when I met these ladies, and call this crazy, I felt that Debra had arranged the whole thing. I always believed, and still do to this day, that Debra was an angel who was sent to me in my time of need. I believe that with every bone and fiber in my body and nothing will ever change my mind. Anyway, we had a great dinner and good conversation. We were quickly becoming friends. We all hung out with each other for the rest of the cruise and on the last day Kristina and I exchanged phone numbers. Kristina was living in Cape Coral, Florida, at the time, and of course, I was in Los Angeles. We started having long phone conversations which helped us in getting to know each other a little better. One day, I was on a ship that had a stop in Key West. As we were docking, Kristina called me and said things that I wondered how she knew. She said, "I called you because I knew the ship was docking." What I didn't know was Kristina had driven 5 hours to meet me as I came off the ship. What a delightful surprise. We had an amazing day together in Key West and it was obvious we cared about each other. I made several trips to Florida and met Kristina's daughters, her son was living in Virginia and I got to meet him sometime later in our relationship. The girls were awesome. Kristina came to LA to scope it out and to get a feel for southern California. At this point in our lives, things just fell into place. We quickly fell madly in love and five months later, on May 15, 2015, Kristina and I got married in Las Vegas by (wait for it) Elvis Presley. Some people may believe that was too soon, but as I had stated before I felt in my heart that this was all arranged by an angel named Debra and I will go to my grave believing that. Let me tell you about Kristina. She's beautiful inside and out. She's sweet, kind, warm and friendly, and loves life. She's smart, amazing at her job, a great mother and an amazing wife, and she has a laugh that's like sweet music to my ears, and she loves to laugh. She is a great lady and I feel so blessed that I get to spend the rest of my life with her. There are not enough words in the English language to describe how fantastic she is, and I will love her with all my heart until I breathe my last breath. As I'm writing this, Kristina and I have been married for over four years and it has been a beautiful marriage. Thanks to my angel Debra!!

Chapter 22

While I was working at the racetrack, the British Invasion, musically speaking, had arrived in the U.S. There were groups like the Searchers, the Dave Clarke 5, the Rolling Stones, and of course the Beatles. At that time, my friends all said I looked like Ringo Starr the drummer of the Beatles. As I got caught up Beatlemania, I thought I should learn to play the drums and start my own group. I began taking lessons from an older gentleman named "Yank" Ragosta who was the house drummer at a Providence R.I. supper club called the "El Morocco". He was a great teacher and in a few short months I was playing drums in local bands and all the while trying to form my own group. I was extremely busy working days at the racetrack and performing at night. I did get to organize a group of musicians into a band and we were called the "Desperados". We had a guitar player, a bass player, lead singer and I played the drums. We stayed together for approx. a year. We got to work a few gigs and recorded a demo. Gradually the band began unraveling. The Lead singer got married, the base player got drafted (Vietnam)and the guitar player decided to move on. One guy I met at the music store where I was taking lessons was Dave Rossi. He was a good drummer and as I recall he had tremendously fast hands. His idol was Buddy Rich. As we became friends, we would practice together at his house and hang out together. One day he told me that Buddy Rich was performing at Lennie's On the Turnpike, a Jazz Club on Route One in Peabody Massachusetts. Dave wanted to go to that show, so he asked me if I would like to go with him. I said "yes I would" David was a couple of years older and it was decided that we would be going in his car which was a no brainer because I had a car at the time that probably wouldn't make it from Providence to Massachusetts. What happened next was mind-boggling. David was a hot young drummer and he had a huge opinion of his drumming ability. During Buddy Rich's set, David started saying how he could play like Buddy and one point he said to me "I want to challenge him to a drum battle." David, although cocky about his drumming was a really shy person. So, he asked me if I go to Buddy after his set and say to him "my friend wants to challenge you to a drum battle". Now, at the time I was young and brazen and certainly foolish, so I agreed to do it. After Buddy Rich finished his set he was tinkering with his drum kit when I approached him out of the blue without even introducing myself and I blurted out "my friend is a great young drummer and would like to challenge you to a drum battle." To this day I have a hard time describing the look on Buddy Rich's face when I said that to him. If you know anything about Buddy Rich, you know he had quite an acerbic personality. Buddy's initial reaction was a feigned laugh. Then he took a few seconds and repeated what I told him, followed by a verbal tirade loaded with expletives. It was one of the silliest things I've ever done. Reflecting on it now, I realize how ridiculous it was for me or David to honestly think that perhaps the greatest drummer of all time would accept such an absurd proposal. Imagine, me asking Buddy Rich to a drum battle on behalf of my friend was akin to an art student challenging Picasso to a paint-off.

Chapter 23

Life sometimes can be so amazing. It can blow your mind. Let me explain. When I was a young teenager, I fell in love with Frankie Valli and the Four Seasons. I bought every record and album I could afford and had pictures of the group hanging in my bedroom. I first got to see the group in person at a county fair in Massachusetts. Believe it or not, when the concert ended some of the members of the group started taking off their neckties as they were about to enter a limousine. I feverishly had worked my way down to a fence just a few feet from the limo and started yelling "Throw me your tie!" Well, Tommy DiVito and Nick Massi both flung their neckties in my direction and I was lucky enough to grab them before anyone else could.

I remember being careful not to mix them up, so as soon as I could I initialed in pen which tie was which. I was so excited and when I got home, I immediately hung them on the wall in my room. The second time I saw the group in person was at Lincoln Downs racetrack. They were performing in the Massachusetts area and they were invited to hand out a trophy to the winning owner of the featured race of the day. The group had a table in the executive turf club. I was working in the stables at the time, and when I heard about them being there I was determined to get up to the turf club to see them. I managed to sneak my way through the crowd and into the turf club and there they were: Frankie Valli, Bob Gaudio, Tommy DiVito, and Nick Massi. I couldn't believe my eyes. I gingerly approached the table and said how much I loved their music., They thanked me and off I ran, because I wasn't supposed to be in the turf club without a pass plus I was too young to be there in the first place. In the years that followed, whenever I had the chance, I would attend their shows. Colleges, supper clubs, special events, I followed them any time they were within driving distance. I guess I was a Four Seasons groupie. All I knew was that I just loved the group's music and Frankie's incredible voice. Once I became a comedian, I always wished I could somehow open their show. I remember going to their concerts and they always had a comic open for them. As I watched the comedian open the show I would picture myself up on that stage. It's strange how I imagined myself on that stage without even remotely thinking of my dream because at that point in my life it had been forgotten. Well, like I said, life can be amazing. In 1988, I got a call from Barry Katz. He booked me to open for Frankie Valli and the Four Seasons at the Paramount Theater in Springfield, Massachusetts. Can you even imagine how I felt? I couldn't put it into words. To me it was a miracle.

I remember feeling this tidal wave of emotion when I met Frankie in the green room. I got the opportunity to chat with him for several minutes about the venue and the show. Then I told him how much of a fan I was and how I followed him throughout the years long before I was a comedian. I even mentioned Lincoln Downs, The County Fair, and the necktie caper. I'm not sure if he remembered but we both had a good laugh. Finally, I went out and did my show. It was a great crowd and I had a great set. After I walked off stage, or should I say floated, I watched in awe as Frankie Valli took the stage. He was magnificent and the band was incredible. It was a glorious night and today it remains as one of the biggest thrills of my career. However, it didn't end there. I was honored to open for Frankie and the Four Seasons several more times and it was always something special. One week, while I was touring with "Dice", we were booked at Bally's in Las Vegas. We had the 10:00 show and guess who had the 8:00 show? Frankie Valli and the Four Seasons. It was so great to see Frankie again and we hung out in the green room after his show and he said he was going to stick around and watch our show. As the years passed, Frankie and I have crossed paths several more times and it was always great. But nothing could ever replace that first time we worked together. Yes, everyone, dreams do come true.

Before performing on cruise ships, I was a road comic for twelve years. Mostly in and around the New England area, however, I would also perform at comedy clubs across the country including places like Ohio,

Michigan, Illinois, Wisconsin, Iowa, Pennsylvania, as well as New York, New Jersey, and Las Vegas. I worked with many different comics at these venues and often, I would be asked the question, "Do you want to get high?" Generally, I would decline in an almost apologetic way.

Now, all my friends and people who know me know I never drank; I never smoked or took drugs of any kind.

So, after being asked if I want to get high so many times I came up with this response, "No thanks, I'm high on life" and that would end that. Sadly, drugs and alcohol played a major role in many comics losing their lives because of it. One encounter sticks out in my mind. There was this young comic who came to Boston from Pittsburgh. I will not divulge his name, but I will say he has the same name as an ex-fiery baseball manager. Anyway, occasionally I would bump into him on the comedy trail.

One day I got a call from a Boston agent named Bill Downs to headline a show in Cape Cod and Bill asked if I could pick up the opening act. I agreed and it was the young comic from Pittsburgh. We arrived at the gig, which was a seedy lounge that featured mostly bands, but they decided they wanted a comedy night. Remember this was the late 80's and comedy had exploded so much so that there were literally a show on every corner. Sadly, there were a portion of them that were hell gigs. When we arrived, the bar manager told us we would spend the night in the band house which was a worn-down shack. The inside looked like a squatter's residence. We did the show, it went ok, I went back to the shack and the young comic stayed at the bar. The next morning, I needed to leave early so I woke him up and he looked like he hadn't slept all night. I told him I needed to get back, he grabbed his stuff and we headed out.

Shortly after leaving, he pulled out a small plastic bag with a little bit of white powder in it. I went ballistic. I told him how dare you to bring that in my car. He said, "I'll get rid of it". So, he snorted whatever was left in the bag and tossed the empty bag out the window. It was a scary experience and the first time I had ever seen anything like that.

Several years after I moved to Los Angeles, I found out that this young comic had become the head writer for a popular television show. I was glad to hear he had turned his life around and I congratulate his success.

In September 1987, I got the opportunity to open for The Beach Boys at Cawley Stadium in Lowell, Massachusetts. It was a live event in the afternoon and there were over 13,000 people in attendance. The show was booked by a Boston comedy booker, Mike Clarke, who happens to be the brother of comedian Lenny Clarke. Mike was also booking several comedy clubs in the Boston area. There were other acts on the bill as well as the Beach Boys. The other acts included The Stompers, Michael McDonald of the Doobie Brothers. The format was for a comic to open for each act. The comics were Jon Pinette, Anthony Clark (no relation to Mike), Jackie Flynn, and me. When the other comics got to the venue, they started to get second thoughts. As for me, it was a grueling trip to get there. The night before I was booked to perform at Niagara University in upstate New York, close to the Canadian border and Niagara Falls. I wanted very much to do the show in Lowell, so I contacted a Rhode Island comic named "Major Tom" and asked if he would come with me to Niagara and help with the drive back to Massachusetts. I told him I would pay him, and he could do a 10-minute spot at the university and it would look good on his resume. He agreed. The show in Niagara went great. Tom and I shared the drive on the way back, each sleeping for an hour or so. Also, as part of the deal Tom would be my guest at the concert which he thought would be really cool. We arrived at the stadium a little early and shortly thereafter the comics began arriving as well. Once everyone was there, Mike Clarke called us together and he laid out the order. Jackie Flynn would open the show, followed by the Stompers, and Anthony Clark would open for Michael McDonald, an intermission, then Jon Pinette would do a spot followed by me, and then the Beach Boys. As the crowd swelled, one by one the comics began suffering from a severe case of cold feet. I might point out that this was a pro bono show with the only compensation being promotional, and to secure a solid spot on Mike's roster. So, backing out was not breaking any contractual obligations. While the other comics were deciding what to do, a member of Michael McDonald's entourage came to Mike Clarke and stated, "Mr. McDonald prefers not to have a comedian perform in front of him". The entire concept of having comedians started to quickly unravel. Looking out at the massive crowd and the atmosphere of an outdoor concert the other comics went to Mike Clarke told him they had decided to leave, giving the reason as it is a guaranteed bomb situation and they wanted no part of it. After they had walked out, Mike came to me and said, "You aren't going to bail on me too" I said, "no way." Mike said, "great, you'll open for the Beach Boys". You see, I saw the whole situation in a different light than the other comics. I figured I had nothing to lose, if I bombed it would be almost certainly expected, but if I somehow did well, I would be a big winner. Plus, either way, I'd stay in good graces with Mike Clarke for future bookings. The Beach Boys arrived while I was on stage, so I never got to meet them. Besides, I couldn't stay for their show and meet them afterwards because I had a college gig that night in New Hampshire. Now here is the best part of the story: just before I was to be introduced the sound system went out. The tech guys were trying desperately to get it fixed and for over a half an hour all you could hear was "check one-two, test one-two." The huge crowd was getting restless, to say the least. I began thinking that my set might get cut out or even the rest of the concert would be canceled. I was getting fidgety. Finally, after what seemed like an eternity, the host, a local radio DJ named Judy Paparelli introduced me; I grabbed my prop bag and hit the stage.

My opening line was "How many people out there never want to hear these words ever again: check one two, test one-two?" The enormous crowd erupted, and I knew I was on my way. I did all my prop bits and the crowd was going wild. I finished with my classic at the time, Tina Turner bit, and the response was amazing. Mike was happy and congratulated me as I left to head up to New Hampshire. The show drew rave reviews in the newspaper and the word spread throughout the comedy community that I had killed in front 13,000 plus people. Believe it or not every so often, even to this day, that show will come up in conversation with many of the Boston comedians. I recall feeling electrified about my performance, but I was a little disappointed I couldn't stick around to watch the Beach Boys show and to meet and greet Al Jardine and Mike Love, the only remaining original band members. However, things have a way of going full circle. Turn the clock ahead 25 years and I get a call to open for Al Jardine who was touring with his own group The Endless Summer Band. I got to hang out with Al, and he is a great guy. I brought up the show at Cawley Stadium and he graciously said he remembered. I went on to tell him that I opened for him on that show and mentioned that it was a big thrill. He kindly thanked me for doing it. What an awesome night. Show business is such an unusual business that you never really know where the next phone call or next audition may lead you. Thus far in my career, I have opened for over 130 national acts in both music and comedy and each one of those shows was an amazing and incredible experience. However, now and then one sticks out in your mind and I must admit that what happened on that September afternoon in Lowell and subsequently 25 years later is one that is still very vivid in my mind.

Chapter 24

It was the 4th of July weekend in the late 80's and I had the great pleasure of opening for Bobby Vinton at the Casino Ballroom in Hampton Beach, New Hampshire. It was an extremely hot and humid night and shortly before showtime, the air conditioning in the venue went out, making the room a sweltering inferno. The staff was trying to solve the AC issue, but after almost an hour, it was determined that it just couldn't be fixed. So, to alleviate some of the heat the staff opened all the outer doors to let some fresh air in. I met Bobby Vinton in the green room, and he was genuinely nice as we discussed the current situation. Finally, management decided to go on with the show and I went out and did a 30-minute set and although the crowd was great, I came off stage looking like I had walked through a car wash. I was soaking wet. And to make matters worse, due to the doors being open, we could hear fireworks going off. And they were loud. It sounded like a war zone. When I got backstage Bobby was there waiting to be introduced and he took one look at me and said, "Oh boy, this is going to be a fun night." I stuck around to watch Bobby's show. His show went great as most of the crowd waited to see him and he didn't disappoint. As he came off stage, and like me earlier, Bobby was drenched. We chatted for a few moments. I thanked him for the chance to open for him and expressed I was a huge fan. Several years later, in the early 90's I happened to be working in Las Vegas at the Comedy Stop at the Tropicana. I had my girlfriend at the time, Felicia, with me. After my late show, Felicia and I decided to go to Downtown Vegas to take advantage of a breakfast special at the Golden Nugget. As we entered the restaurant, I noticed Bobby Vinton was sitting with a bunch of people, which surprised me because I had no idea that Bobby Vinton was in town let alone performing at the Golden Nugget. Felicia and I sat down and once we got settled, I thought I would go over to Bobby's table and say hi, and if he remembered New Hampshire. I introduced myself and told Bobby I was working at the Tropicana and I mentioned our little episode in New Hampshire. He immediately remembered and recalled how hot it was. What happened next surprised me. I said to him "I didn't realize you were working in town, he said "yeah, I'm here at the nugget" and he asked me if I would like to come to his show as his guest. I told him I would love to but I'm working seven nights a week at the "Trop", and I couldn't possibly make it. But I said, "my girlfriend is with me and she would love to go, I'm sure". He said, "that would be great" and he gave me his room number at the Golden Nugget and continued "call my manager tomorrow and he will set things up." I said, "thank you Bobby that would be awesome." As I made it back to my table, I told Felicia and she was excited to see the show. She remembered watching Bobby on TV with her mom who was also a big fan. The next day I called Bobby's room and his manager, who was at Bobby's table the night before, answered the phone. I introduced myself and said, "Bobby told me to call regarding his show tonight". What happened next really shocked me, believe me, I didn't see this coming. The manager bluntly said, "unfortunately, the show has been sold out." I was so surprised that all I could say was "Okay, thank you." I was disappointed and knowing Bobby Vinton only for a short time he seemed to me to be an honest and sincere guy. I apologized to Felicia and told her I felt like I had let her down. About half an hour later, the phone rings in our hotel room and it's Bobby Vinton's manager. What was about to transpire was utterly amazing. The manager explained "there was a terrible mistake and Bobby wants your girlfriend to come to tonight's show. Bobby is sending a limo to the Tropicana to pick her up at 7:00 pm. Oh, and Bobby wants to say hi." Bobby got on the phone and said, "I'm so sorry, but my manager had made a mistake and then he said, and I kid you not, "she will sit with my daughter at our VIP table and there will be a bottle of champagne there for her." I was rocked. What a classy guy. Bobby Vinton went out of his way to make sure that my girlfriend Felicia was taken care of. Like I had stated earlier, I have worked with so many celebrities and 99.9% of them are great people. But occasionally you work with one that leaves a lasting impression. Bobby Vinton is certainly one of them. A true down to earth gentleman in every respect.

Again, in the late '80s, when I was commuting to New York and eventually living there, I got the opportunity to perform at Rodney Dangerfield's club called, what else, Dangerfield's. It was a great comedy club with all you would expect from a New York City comedy room. Checkered tablecloths with a candle on them, tables and chairs packed in close together, dim dank lighting, and a really small stage. It was perfect and I performed there many times and got to meet the man Rodney Dangerfield on numerous occasions. I must tell you, off stage he was exactly what you would see on stage. If you have seen the movie "Caddy Shack" that movie pretty much was Rodney in real life, a real character. He would always call me "kid." When I would see him in his club, he would always say, "Hey kid, how you are doing?" Many times, he would come into the bar area of the club in his bathrobe and kid and joke around with the comics and staff. He was hilarious. After I moved out of New York I would go back and do Rodney's club, perhaps once or twice a year. so, I hadn't seen much of him again until I started working in Las Vegas. What I didn't know was that after his comedy room, called Rodney's Place, closed at the Old El Rancho in Vegas, Rodney had his show for a while at the Tropicana in the very same room that the Comedy Stop was in. One night while performing at the Comedy Stop, something crazy happened. I had just finished my headliner show and went back to the green room. What I didn't know was Rodney Dangerfield saw my name on the marquee, and decided to stop in to watch my show, and perhaps do a few minutes on stage. Suddenly, Rodney walks into the green room and said, "Hey kid, really funny show." Rodney was there with his beautiful young wife and she also said she enjoyed my show. I thanked them for coming but what I didn't know trouble was brewing. As we were chatting, Rodney mentioned that he wanted to do a few minutes of his act for old time's sake because after all, it was his old room. However, the owner Bob Kephart, who also books all the shows, refused to let Rodney go on because he was leery Rodney would use some bad language. If you had only seen Rodney on TV variety shows or Late-Night talk shows or network specials, you would see only clean material from Rodney. But live or on cable, Rodney wasn't bashful about using strong R- rated language and Kephart feared that would happen if he let Rodney go on. I should also mention Kephart had a ban on using the "F" bomb which also heightened the situation. In the green room, Rodney was really upset. He couldn't believe Kephart wouldn't put him on. Rodney promised he would work clean but Kephart wouldn't give in. Finally, Rodney realized Kephart wouldn't relent, So, we said our good byes, Rodney walked out of the club and that was the last time I saw Rodney Dangerfield alive. I could always relate to Rodney because, like me, he started his career later in life and made it to the top and I always admired the fact that Rodney never gave up and that kind of determination is inside of me.

Another facet of my career was opening for musical icons. It was something special for me to open for them because it was their music that I've loved and listened to long before I was a comedian. Groups like the Guess Who, and their lead singer Burton Cummings, who to this day remains one of my favorites. One particular afternoon I got a call from my agent with an offer to open for the Guess Who in a 600-seat banquet room, at a hotel in Harrisburg, Pennsylvania. The group was without Burton Cummings, who left in 1975 to embark on a solo career. I believe there was one or perhaps two original members in the group that night. Although I never really knew for sure. As I recall, the room was filled, and they were a fantastic crowd. I can honestly tell you I received a standing ovation for my 30-minute set. The local DJ who hosted the show took me off stage and then introduced the Guess Who. They were phenomenal. I stayed out front to watch their show and I must admit, the thrill of getting a standing ovation and the amazing show put on by the Guess Who made it a night I will always consider as one of the biggest highlights of my career.

People like Chubby Checker who I remember when I was a young teenager trying to learn the latest dance craze called "The Twist "by using a bath towel. Then some 20 odd years later opening for him at a New England college. At the time I was still doing props and a photo was taken with me just coming off stage wearing a jean skirt, pink leotards, and bright red lipstick. Upon finishing my show with my Tina Turner impression, as the photo shows, Chubby was slightly perplexed, but we laughed about it later. It was a great thrill.

Chapter 25

I had the opportunity to open for Ben Vereen several times and each time he was such a gentleman and great to work with aside from being an incredibly talented performer. In fact, we worked so well together that his manager and I had talks about me opening for Ben on a regular basis. Although that never came to fruition, there was one night which I will never forget. I had finished my set and was watching Ben's show for approximately ten minutes when out of nowhere in a darkened theater an audience member had arrived late and walked down the aisle and across the front of the stage. Well, this did not sit well with Ben. Shockingly, Ben abruptly stopped his show and began to read this audience member the riot act. Ben said, and I'm somewhat paraphrasing, "How dare you cross in front of the stage during my show. Every person who is on stage performing is an artist and to disrupt or distract their performance is rude and disrespectful and don't you ever do such a thing again." The crowd was stunned. After what seemed like a life time of silence, Ben continued his show. It was a scene I'll soon not forget.

One weekend, back in the 90's, I got booked at Nick's Comedy Stop in Boston to open for Jimmie Walker, who achieved fame as J.J. on the hit TV show "Good Times." I met Jimmie in the green room, and he was friendly and funny as we joked around with each other. After finishing my set, I headed back to the green room, gathered myself and walked out to a packed house of approximately 400 people to watch Jimmie's show. And to my surprise, expecting to hear Dy-no-mite, Jimmie opened his show by telling the audience he wasn't going to say it. Judging by the audience's reaction they weren't happy to hear that. I would assume that if you pay to see Jimmie Walker, you will want to hear that famous expression of him saying "Dy-no-mite." It was kind of a shock to me as well as the audience that night. The following night in the green room things seemed normal as we chatted, but I never did ask him why he wouldn't say "Dy-no-mite."

Regis Philbin and his wife Joy loved cruising and one week as I was headlining on a Celebrity cruise ship, Regis and Joy were also on board for the 7-day cruise. Regis was scheduled to do a matinee show singing and playing the piano and do a session of his game show "Who Wants to be a Millionaire" which was extremely popular at the time. He was also scheduled to do a Q+A in the showroom on another afternoon during the cruise. After Regis had done his main show of singing and playing the piano, I went backstage to say hello and congratulate him on his performance. I recall at one-point during his millionaire segment he began talking to a lady in the audience, I don't recall her name, but let's just say for the sake of the story her name was "Judy". While Regis was talking to the woman, he kept calling her let's say "Mary" and the crowd kept calling out "Judy." After the show while we were backstage, Regis kept insisting to me that he was calling the woman by her right name, which I swear he wasn't. He continued to tell me that it was her right name and I'm telling him it wasn't. Regis was being Regis through this entire episode and we both had great fun with it. I enjoyed working with him; he certainly is one of a kind.

It was 1987, only two years into my comedy career, when Barry Katz started to book me in all of the comedy rooms he had at that time. One day while Barry and I were having lunch he told me he was working on bringing in Henny Youngman to do a show at Symphony Hall in Boston. During lunch he offered me the spot of hosting the show. I was overly excited because when I was a teenager working at the racetrack, Henny Youngman was at Narragansett Park to make a presentation to the winning owner of the featured race. The presentation took place in front of the Grandstand in the winner's circle. As a brazen young teenager, I pushed my way through the crowd as Mr. Youngman was leaving the winner's circle and approached him and told him my dream was to become a standup comedian. I said that because seeing him in person relit the spark to my dream. He was very gracious and sincere, he then pulled out his business card and said to me, "send me your address and I'll send you a copy of my book." I was elated. I couldn't wait to mail him my information. His card listed his address in New York, so the very next day I wrote a thank you letter with my address on it. Back then I couldn't stop thinking about Mr. Youngman sending me a copy of his book. As I learned through years of experience, not everyone in the entertainment business follows up with actions regarding their words. Sure enough, at some point not too long after I sent my letter to Mr. Youngman, his book arrived in the mail. I was overjoyed. I opened the package and there was a handwritten note on a page in the book wishing me good luck. Much to my sadness, I no longer have that book. Somehow with all the changes I have gone through, the book got lost in the shuffle. Barry Katz had called me to inform me that the show at Symphony Hall was a go. Barry had booked a Boston comic named Johnathan Katz (no relation to Barry) as the featured act. I was to open the show with a seven-minute spot, bring on Jonathan, and after his spot of approximately 20-30 minutes, I got to introduce Henny Youngman. Here I am, a former used car dealer, introducing a comedy legend. Again, words fall short of describing how I felt. I spoke with Mr. Youngman briefly before the show and mentioned what had happened at a Rhode Island racetrack (Narragansett Park) some 25 years earlier and I thanked him for it. I didn't expect him to remember and I'm not sure if he did, but he said he did and was glad he could help. What an incredible experience to have shared the stage with the great Henny Youngman. It was people like him and many other comics of that era that were the foundation my dream was built upon. However, the story doesn't end yet. Roughly five years later, I got a call from a Boston booking agent who had hired Henny Youngman to perform at a large banquet hall inside a huge steakhouse in Northern Massachusetts. The booker asked me if I would be interested in opening for him. I happily accepted. The night of the show I arrived 15 minutes before showtime and headed to the green room. At that point, Mr. Youngman hadn't arrived. It was now show time and no sign of Henny Youngman. I went out on stage and started my set. At approximately 30 minutes into my act I noticed Henny in the wings. I wrapped up my set and the audience was great. It was then my duty to introduce Henny Youngman. I made the introduction and as I left the stage, I noticed that Mr. Youngman was sitting in a wheelchair. His people then wheeled him on stage and attempted to place him on a chair. It was a very awkward situation as Mr. Youngman and his handlers lost their grip and Mr. Youngman nearly fell as the crowd gasped. After a second effort, Henny was secure in his chair and began his act. Once he started, a gentleman (I'm not sure if it was his son) was sitting on the floor holding cue cards. It was heartbreaking to see this, even with the aid of the cue cards, Henny Youngman repeated his famous tagline "take my wife, please" nearly a dozen times. He stumbled through his set and was gingerly placed back in his wheelchair. What happened next was utterly amazing, Henny Youngman received a standing ovation and dozens of adoring fans rushed to the wheelchair to say thank you and what many felt would be a final goodbye. I had chills running up and down my spine watching this unbelievable sight unfold. After a while, Henny Youngman was wheeled out of the building. While nearly everyone who was in attendance was still standing around, I noticed there wasn't a dry eye among them. Sadly, like so many other celebrities and athletes, Henny Youngman stuck around a little too long. However, to me he will always be an inspirational part of my career. He was without a doubt a true comedy icon. God bless Henny Youngman.

After being released from the federal institution and getting my career back on track, Charlie Hall, a Rhode Island comic who was a tremendous help in building my career, called me in the spring 1991, and asked me to be a part of an all-star show at the Warwick Musical Theater. The show featured Pat Benatar, John Secada, Adam Ant, Corey Hart, among others. The plan for the show was to have a comic open for each act. Back in the 1950s, the Warwick Musical Theatre was originally a huge tent with musicals being the featured shows. In the '70s, the theater was renovated into an indoor three thousand-three hundred seat theater in the round. The owner was a man named "Buster" Bonoff. Some of the biggest acts in show business performed there in the '70s, '80s, and even into the '90s. A partial list of the acts that performed there were Liberace, Tony Bennett Tom Jones, Sammy Davis Jr., Don Rickles and many more. The show I'm referring to was an afternoon show, and it drew a packed house. My spot was to open for John Secada. John was a former backup singer to Gloria Estefan and now was performing as a solo artist. He went on to release his first album, "Jon Secada", which sold over 6 million copies. As the comedians and I gathered in the green room a man entered and told us what the lineup would be. This man was wearing a sleeveless shirt, a black leather vest, and had the perfect look of a biker or a roadie, including a "Born to Raise Hell" tattoo. As he was talking, I jumped in with my idea of having the comedians go first, and then the musical acts to close the show. Well, this idea didn't sit well and in no uncertain terms, he let me know we were going to do it his way. As he walked away, I asked Charlie, "Who was that guy?" Charlie told me it was Larry Bonoff, (Buster's son) the owner and CEO of the Warwick Musical Theater. After that show, I tried on numerous occasions to call Larry and to apologize but I never got him on the phone. After more than a year of trying, I finally got him to answer my call. He didn't say hello, he didn't reprimand me, and I didn't even get the chance to apologize. The first words out of his mouth were, "do you think you've suffered enough?" I was taken aback, but I said, "Yes I have." He then said, "Okay this weekend you're opening for Huey Lewis and the News." I said, "thank you" and that was that. After the Huey Lewis show Larry and I began building a friendship and I became a regular opener for numerous celebrities over the next seven to eight years. Eventually, feeling the pressure of the adjacent Foxwoods and Mohegan Sun Casinos, the Warwick Musical Theater closed its doors for good in 1999 and was demolished in 2002, An incredibly sad ending for an iconic show business venue. Larry finally sold the property and today sitting on the land that was once trod upon by some of the most famous people in show business history is a Lowe's home improvement store!

Chapter 26

The '90s was an awesome decade for me. Opening for national acts, doing movies, and meeting Debra. Unfortunately, my relationship with Felicia came to a sad ending. Also, in the 90's I did two live New Year's Eve Celebrations on Comcast cable from Disneyworld in Florida. My New York agent Dee had negotiated the contracts for the show. It was a little strange how I got the show. I was a regular headliner at the Comedy Connection in East Providence, Rhode Island. One night after my show I was approached by Joe Rocco, who was the sports anchor on the NBC affiliate in Providence. Joe had a connection with Comcast and was looking for comedians to perform on a New Year's Eve special which would be broadcast live from the Superstar Theater in Disney World. Joe asked if I would do it and I said "absolutely". It was an incredible experience. And it was live! The host of the show was comedian Jeff Ross who you may know from the Comedy Central Roasts. I was dressed in shorts and a silly top when I arrived at the Superstar Theater for hair and makeup. I had brought an outfit for the show but when the director saw what I was, he thought it would be great to wear on the show. The backdrop I would be performing in front of was a Gilligan's Island set complete with the damaged "Minnow" so that's what prompted the director to go with my outfit. The show went great and the audience was amazing. I did so well I was asked back for the following year as the show's co-host. It was quite an honor. Those shows were definitely one of the highlights of my career. One for the fact that it was live TV and two for the thrill of doing it at the Superstar Theater in Disney World. For reasons I was not privy to, the show only had a brief run. The '90s caused another breakup, this time with my New York agent. I told her I was moving to LA and I thought that with me being in LA and she being in New York it would make it extremely difficult to continue to work together. I knew it would be nearly impossible, without the technology of today, for her to meet with managers and casting directors as well as any industry people who wanted to sit down face to face and negotiate. So, sadly, we ended our working relationship. We had a good run. Venues such as Major Corporate events, Cruise Ships, commercials, and film were all made possible by her tireless effort and her belief in my talent. Also, in the 90's I continued to pursue hosting and I successfully booked various local commercials. One I recall fondly. I was asked to be the spokesperson for all the Rhode Island lottery commercials. We did many different spots with me as a character in various sketches. It was really a lot of fun to do them.

The 90's for me was a jam-packed decade of doing live TV, feature films, sporting events, a spokesperson for the lottery, the host of "On Location with the Mayor of Providence" headlining in Las Vegas, Atlantic City, opening for national acts at the Warwick Musical Theater as well as many other venues including Disney World. I was now a local celebrity and I felt I had done all I could accomplish in Rhode Island and the New England area and it was time to stop being a big fish in a small pond, but to dive headfirst into the Pacific Ocean. So, with all that behind me, I believed I was ready to compete on the world's largest stage, Hollywood, California.

In the early nineties, I was a regular headliner at the Comedy Stop in Las Vegas, as well as The Comedy Stop in Atlantic City. On one particular Las Vegas booking, a one-week headlining engagement, I was booked with a comic-magician named Levent and the feature act was a comic from Ohio named Drew Carey. It was quite a week. Right from opening night there was tension between the two of them. It seems that Levent was unhappy with the behavior of Drew Carey because he thought that Drew was making fun of him and his act. Let me explain, Levent would close his show with a magic trick that was sucking a potted plant up his nose. It was a funny bit. When he finished his act with the plant trick, Levent would walk off stage then Drew would be introduced by the local host. Levent would stick around and watch the show. Now here's where the tension arose. Drew would walk on stage, take the microphone and say, "Let's have a hand for Levent" and then he would say "Yeah, great, sucking a potted plant up his nose" and with that make a hand gesture like he was masturbating. Well, Levent didn't take too kindly to this and as the headliner he came to me and asked if I would talk to Carey about this. So, I pulled Drew aside the following night and told him Levent was upset about being made fun of and asked Drew if he would stop. Drew said to me sarcastically, "Hey, he is sucking a potted plant up his nose." I said, "Drew, we will be here the whole week and we shouldn't have tension like this." Drew then said, "Okay, I won't do it anymore" and he didn't, and the rest of the week things went great. And that was the end of that.

While I was touring with "Dice" as his opening act we had a regular gig at Bally's in Las Vegas several times a year. We had a booking in May of 1994 and while we were there, Frank Sinatra was headlining at the MGM Grand. "Dice" was a huge fan of Sinatra and planned to go to Frank's show. As it turned out Frank's show would start one hour earlier than our show as we generally would do a later show in Vegas. The plan was laid out that "Dice" would go see Frank and scurry back to do our show. "Dice" told me to stay on stage until I spot him in the wings. Now all the logistics were in place. I recall doing my show and all the while glancing off stage to see if "Dice" had arrived. It was around the thirty-minute mark and still no sign of "Dice". At approximately forty-minutes into my set I spotted "Dice", so I immediately went into my closing bit and finished my set. I then introduced him, and he headed out to the center stage. Now at this point, I had been opening for him for over a year and over one hundred shows, I could tell he just wasn't himself. I'm sure his audience couldn't tell but I knew something just wasn't right. "Dice" finished his set and we all went back to his suite, which ironically was the Sinatra Suite at Bally's. I asked him how Frank's show went and that was when things began to unravel. "Dice" became very emotional as he explained how Frank Sinatra a man he adored as an entertainer, had trouble remembering the words to his songs, how Frank would stop in the middle of a song, not knowing where he was or what song he was singing. As "Dice" continued to explain what happened, he started to break down. He went on about how sad he felt and how devastating it was to watch. By this time, "Dice" was intensely upset. Dice's road manager "Hot Tub"

Johnnie, and others in our entourage also felt emotional. I must admit it was one of the saddest moments of my career. I remember I wanted to go to see Frank with "Dice", but because of our show schedules, I was unable to. In hindsight, I'm glad I didn't see the show. I witnessed that scenario with Henny Youngman, and I didn't want to see something like that again. I'm happy that I can remember Frank Sinatra as one of the biggest icons in the history of show business.

In 1996, while still living in Rhode Island, I was auditioning regularly for a casting company called Collinge-Pickman, who at the time were the biggest casting agents in Boston. They got me an audition with casting director, Ferne Cassel, who had cast big-budget movies including "Taken" "Predator 2" and "Demolition man"

She loved my audition and said to me "do you know what you just did" I said something like "I think so." I must have done something right because I booked the movie. It was titled "Celtic Pride" which was written by Judd Apatow and starred Dan Aykroyd and featured basketball greats Larry Bird and Bill Walton. The other film I auditioned for in 1996 was a movie called. "The Mouse." The casting directors were Walken-Jaffe. Georgianne Walken (who happens to be Christopher Wilken's wife) and Sheila Jaffe. Together they have cast many major motion pictures including "The Italian Job" "Entourage" "Ted" and "The Fighter" to name a few. It was a movie based on the real life of a prizefighter named Bruce "Mouse" Strauss. He was the ultimate opponent, losing almost all of his fights to the local boxing hero. The audition went great and I was cast for the role of Don, a boxing promoter. Here were my scenes. "Don" is at the fights and is frantic because his fighter has not shown up and his fighter's bout is next up. Luckily, Don spots the "Mouse" in the crowd who was just there watching the fights. "Don" approaches the Mouse and desperately tries to convince him to fill in for his fighter, the Mouse says, "I can't take a chance, I'm getting knocked out in a couple of days in Las Vegas." So, Don promises the "Mouse" that the local hero would not throw any left hooks. "Mouse" agrees to do it under those conditions. So, we have a meeting with the local fighter's handlers and the local boy's manager, played by the boxing icon Angelo Dundee, objects in a way only Angelo Dundee could. Finally, after much bickering, all parties agreed. It was a fun and exciting project. The movie had an amazing cast. It starred John Savage as the "Mouse" and there were many boxing notables in the movie as well. Vito Antuofermo, Randall "Tex" Cobb, Ray "Boom, Boom" Mancini, and several others. Rip Torn was also featured in the film, and he was great. It was an awesome shoot and equally awesome to meet some of the professional fighters as well as Muhammad Ali's trainer, the great Angelo Dundee. It was an experience I will never forget. Quick note: 10 years after the movie I met John Savage at an after-party for Fred Travalena, who had just received his star on the Hollywood Walk of Fame. The party was held at a 20-million-dollar mansion in the Hollywood Hills owned by entrepreneur and animal activist, Robert Lohse. One of the special guests at the party was a real live white tiger.

John and I reminisced about the movie and how much fun it was. John Savage was extremely cordial, and we had a great chat.

Chapter 27

One particular day in the late 90's I get a call from Bill Blumenreich. He asks me about a weekend and if I'm available. A quick check of my calendar shows that I am, so I said "yes, I'm open." He asks if I want to work the weekend with Jamie Foxx. I said "yes, I'd love to" At that time, Jamie had been on "In Living Color" and also had done his breakout movie "Booty Call" I was a big fan of Jamie Foxx and thought this would be a fun weekend. The gig was four shows at the Comedy Connection in Faneuil Hall in Boston. There were two shows on Friday and two shows on Saturday. The room had a 500-seat capacity. I got there early as usual and shortly thereafter Jamie came to the green room. He was very friendly, and we talked about gigs, certain Comedy Clubs, and life on the road. I remember both shows Friday were sold out and we both did great. After the shows, we said a few words and said see you tomorrow. Saturday night both shows again sold out. Jamie and I hung out in the green room and got to know each other a little better. Working with Jamie Foxx was a tremendous thrill and I'm so happy that he has gone on to an amazing career. Jamie Foxx is a good guy and was a pleasure to work with.

A few years after moving to LA I got an offer from a Florida booker to do two weeks touring the retirement communities in Florida. I was booked to open for Rita Moreno.

However, there was a contract dispute between her and the booking agency, so Rita pulled out. The booking agent threatened her with a lawsuit. Rita contacted her attorney and, eventually, both parties came to a settlement, the agreement was Rita Moreno had to perform at least one night to honor her contract and to avoid any legal action against her. The story that I heard was that Rita called her friend, Marvin Hamlisch, to fill in for her. So, as it turned out for the bulk of my contract, I was opening for Marvin Hamlisch. Marvin was a great guy; he was very warm and friendly.

The way the retirement villages worked was to do two locations each night. To pull this off I would do my 1st show, and as I was leaving for my 2nd show, Marvin would be coming in to do his 1st show and then would show up to do his 2nd show as I was finishing my 2nd show. I hope I made that clear enough. So, I would just say hello as we crossed paths. One night, I asked Marvin if we could take a photo together and he said, "Tomorrow night I will come early so we can spend some time and take a few photos." Now, Marvin didn't have to show up until approximately 7:45 for the 7:00 show as I would open with a forty-minute set. but because I asked for the photo, Marvin was at the venue around 6:30 so we could take pictures before I went on stage at 7:00. That, my friends, is a class act. It was a great thrill and honor to work with the incredibly talented and all-around sweet guy, Marvin Hamlisch. The closing night of my engagement was a Saturday. That was the one night that Rita Moreno was obligated to perform. She was there with her husband, and they arrived early. It was even before I went on, and it was obvious that she was not thrilled to be there.

However, I must say she was very friendly to me and to Debra, who was with me on that tour. It was also apparent that Rita wasn't fully prepared for the show. She was having trouble getting her hair right and she had forgotten her earrings.

Debra to the rescue. Being a hairstylist, Debra volunteered to do Rita's hair and let Rita wear her diamond earrings, as you can see in the photo. Rita was grateful, and her and Debra shared some pleasant moments together. As for the shows, they went great and we both got standing ovations, but a funny thing happened when Rita finished. She walked off the stage and planned to go back out for an encore, but when she got to the wings, our driver who was also the booking agent's son- in- law, pushed Rita back out because the crowd was all but gone. It was an awkwardly funny moment. As I look back, I must say it was a tremendous experience to work with a woman who had won an Emmy, a Grammy, an Oscar, and a Tony in a career that has spanned 70 years. I am living my dream.

On December 15th, 1998, I was on the Monarch of The Seas for a one-week engagement. Also performing on the ship that week was comedian John Pinette and magician Greg Gleason. It was an Eastern Caribbean run with several ports of call including St. Thomas and St. Maarten. I recall It was formal night on the ship as we sailed out of St. Thomas. Several hours later, around midnight, we were informed through an announcement by the captain that a medical emergency had occurred. The captain had decided not to turn back to St. Thomas, but to continue to our next port of call, St. Maarten. At that time, St. Maarten did not have a docking pier, so to get on the island, tender boats were needed. St. Maarten is a very tricky island to navigate. It takes great sailing skills to get close enough for the tender boats to safely ferry passengers from the ship to the island. For that reason, and in most similar circumstances, a pilot, someone who knows and understands the waters surrounding the island, would reach the ship in a pilot boat. The pilot would then hop aboard and guide the ship to a safe position, then the captain would drop anchor. But because of the emergency the captain decided to drop anchor on his own. He was able to maneuver the ship, without the aid of a pilot safely into the harbor. The medical staff was able to transport the passenger to the waiting tender boat, which would take the patient to the medical team waiting on the island. That entire process seemed to go very smoothly as Debra and I, as well as many other passengers, watched from deck seven, which was the deck our cabin was on. Once the process was complete, we headed back to our cabin. As Debra and I were preparing for bed, something very strange and unusual happened. We heard a very distinct and unrecognizable noise, which was followed by an eerie silence.

It was something I've never heard before and thought I should go back out and look around. The best way I can describe the noise I heard was that it was like an extremely loud scraping noise. I went back to my cabin and told Debra to come back out with me. A noticeably short time after we got back out on the deck, there were more passengers gathering. Some were dressed formally, and others were in their pajamas. It was surreal. Just then, the ship's alarm sounded seven short blasts and one long blast which means all passengers grab their life jackets and head to their muster stations. This was quickly followed by the captain coming on the public address system to make an announcement. Here's what happened: The captain was turning the ship around when he drove it across a reef, causing a 130-foot gash in the ship's hull. The ship was now taking on water and the massive ship began listing. The safety crew told us that we would have to evacuate the ship. Security had locked down all decks so if you were out of your cabin you could not return, and the passengers in their cabins were forced to leave. What happened next was very unnerving. The safety crew lowered the lifeboats. While this was taking place, the captain kept making announcements in, I might add, a very shaky voice. Just as we were about to enter the lifeboats, the captain came back with an announcement. He had decided to drive the ship on a sandbar to stop the onslaught of water. We would then be able board the tender boats and be transported to the island. Luckily, it worked.

We were led through the crew area and to a staircase and began climbing down the stairs from deck seven. As we got closer, we noticed that deck one and two were completely underwater. There were makeshift platforms to get us on the tender boats. The cruise line was frantically trying to arrange hotels and next day flights. When we got off the tender boats there were vans that took us to the airport, where the cruise line had brought the passengers luggage. The parking lot of the airport was piled high with all sorts of suit cases, duffle bags, and ladies purses. The entire procedure became an absolute nightmare. It was a mob scene, people were pushing and shoving each other to find their belongings. It was a miracle that Debra and I were able to locate our bags through all that. The next step was to secure lodging. In the meantime, the cruise director was trying to restore order but to no avail. The crowd wouldn't listen and continued to wreak havoc. While the chaos continued I spotted a van, so Debra and I pushed through the massive amount of people looking for their luggage and luckily we reached the van in time as the van driver was handing out hotel room keys. I somehow managed to grab a key, hop in the van which took us to a hotel on the island. Debra and I were among the lucky ones as many other passengers slept on the beach. The next morning, we got to the airport bright and early and, even though it was very crowded, we managed to secure our flights home. The nightmare was over. There were many things we lost because of what happened, but through legal channels, we were able to get some back. Not all, but some is better than none. It certainly was a hair-raising experience. As I look back, I recall many people were on the ship's deck sobbing when the lifeboats were lowered. Let me add that Debra was a good swimmer, and even though I swim like a piano, at one point I actually gave a thought of trying to swim to the island. Fear is a powerful emotion. As I write this, I have performed on cruise ships for over 20 years and I will tell you that was the closest call I've ever had. All in all, performing on cruise ships has been a wonderful and amazing experience. The incredible people I've met, the fascinating places I've been to, have made it a part of my career I will always cherish.

Chapter 28

Earlier I mentioned Bob Kephart and I must admit he was not the warmest biscuit in the basket. I also mentioned that he had a no "F" rule in his club. On one particular engagement at the "Comedy Stop at the Trop", I was working with another comic, a very funny guy named Jeff Allen. On opening night, before the show, Jeff came into the green room a little upset when he was informed there was a no "F" rule because he had a bit in his act where he needed to use it to make the joke effective.

He went to Kephart and explained that the only way the bit works is by using the "F" word. Jeff further explained that he had tried the bit using a different word like "screwed", but the bit would fall flat on its face. Jeff further told me that Kephart told him, a rule is a rule, so either do it with a different word or drop the bit.

I was headlining the show and Jeff was the feature, so I got to watch Jeff's set to see what he was going to do with the bit. I had worked with Jeff several times before, so I knew what the bit was. Sure enough, Jeff decided to do the bit and when it came to that point in the bit, Jeff dropped the "F" bomb. Immediately after the show, Kephart fired Jeff Allen. Generally, it was Bob's way or the highway. I also had a run-in with Bob Kephart.

It was the nineties and I was still headquartered in Rhode Island. So, when Kephart would book me in Atlantic City I would make the 5-hour drive without any travel compensation. However, when he booked me in Las Vegas he would include $200 in my check to cover my airfare.

This went on for a while until I finally confronted Bob with an issue. I got him on the phone and explained that I could no longer confirm flights to Las Vegas for $200. Most flights at that time from Providence or Boston to Vegas was in the $300 plus range. So, I asked him if he would be willing to add $100 to my check to cover some of the flight expenses because frankly, I was losing money at $200. We spoke for several minutes and Bob agreed. I arrived in Vegas, got to the hotel, went to my room at the Tropicana, and prepared for my week's engagement. The week went extremely well. Great crowds and I had great shows. After my final performance for the week, as was the custom with Bob, I would go to his office to pick up my check, and he would book my next appearance. That was the drill. When I arrived, he had my check waiting, but when I looked at it, the check did not include the additional $100 for my flights. When I mentioned to Bob that the check was short, he seemed surprised. He said, "What do you mean?" I replied, "Our phone conversation regarding my travel. You agreed to add another $100 to my check to help cover my flights." He laughed at me like I had three heads and said, "I don't remember that conversation." I tried to re-explain myself, but I could sense that he wasn't into what I was saying. After my final plea, he said, "Well, if you say so," and wrote me another check for $100. I thanked him for understanding and then mentioned that I had my calendar. He immediately balked and said, "Well it's late now. Call me tomorrow or when you get a chance and we'll book your next appearance." As I left his office, I knew being the kind of guy he was, internally he was fuming.

However, when I got home and settled, I made numerous calls to Bob, but he would never answer or return my calls.

For the discrepancy of $100, which he agreed to pay, Bob Kephart held a grudge against me for years. My efforts to talk to him and clear the air were in vain. And because of what happened, Bob Kephart never booked me again in any of his clubs, weather it was Las Vegas, Atlantic City, or Laughlin Nevada.

I had the good fortune to open for a lovely and fun lady with a very engaging personality. Her name is Maria Del Rosario Mercedes Pilar Martinez Molina Baeza, better known as "Charo." We did several shows together and she affectionately referred to me as the Marble Man because of the references in my act to marbles. She was a sheer delight to work with and quite a funny character, as well. For a period of time, Charo had her own show in Las Vegas and whenever I was in town, I would let her know and she would invite me to come see her. When I would attend, I would stop backstage and say hi, and then at some point in her act she would say, "I want to say hi to my friend, a very funny comedian, The Marble Man."

It was kind of an inside joke.

What some people may not know about "Charo" is that she is professionally trained and is an extremely accomplished guitarist. Her rendition of Ravel's Bolero on an acoustic twelve string guitar is mesmerizing. It was a great honor and privilege to work with her and get to know her. Underneath the sexy, silly, cuchi-cuchi girl was a solid actress, an incredible musician, and a kind, lovable person.

I got to meet Dave Coulier on the set of the ABC television show "America's Funniest People." Dave was the co-host of the show along with Arlene Sorkin. It was 1991 and I had responded to an ad in a Boston newspaper that the show was looking for people in the Boston area with a funny, unusual talent. I managed to get an audition for the show. I did a five-minute set in which I brought back some of the props I once used in my act. I also included the very first bit I ever did on stage, which was the opening to the old television show Superman that I would recite, twisting the words (spoonerisms). My set was shot in Boston Harbor on one of the original Tea Party ships. Several days later I get a call from the talent coordinator at ABC telling me how much they loved my set and they wanted to book me on the show doing my Superman bit. I was incredibly excited. A couple of weeks later I received an airline ticket and a reservation at the Hilton Hotel in Los Angeles, plus a voucher of five hundred dollars to attend the airing of the show. Once I arrived at the ABC studio, I was taken to the green room to await hair and makeup. Once that was done, I was introduced to Dave and we chatted, mostly about comedy, and he was very cool. I was also introduced to the creator and producer of the show, Vin Di Bona. I had no idea Vin Di Bona and I lived in Rhode Island, at the same time. I lived in Providence and Vin just a few miles away in Cranston Rhode Island. Vin's dad had a successful restaurant in Cranston back in the 60's which I knew about, but I had never attended. My dining experience back then was a series of fast-food chains or more affordable eating establishments. Vin and I talked for a while discussing the coincidence of us living near each other back in Rhode Island. He then told me that if I ever came back to LA to be sure to look him up and in the meantime, he said, "Keep me updated on your career." I corresponded with Vin many times over the years leading up to my move to LA in 2000. Once I was settled in LA, I reached out to Vin again. We had a wonderful phone conversation, and in closing he told me he would set a date for a meeting in his office. A few days later, I got a call from Vin's assistant with a time to come to Vin's Production Company. Vin and I had an outstanding meeting for over an hour talking about his journey from Rhode Island to Los Angeles and the industry in general. From that moment on Vin and I became friends. We would meet for lunch from time to time, and to this day he still follows my career closely as I keep him abreast of my latest projects. One summer in the late 90's the cruise industry was going through a lull in bookings, so I decided to take the summer off from cruise engagements. I spoke to Vin about this and he asked if I would be interested in working for him for the summer as a video screener for his long running TV show, "America's Funniest Videos." I immediately accepted. The job was a blast. I would watch hundreds of outrageous videos and submit to the producers the ones I deemed best for the show. Many of my choices actually made it to the broadcast. Often at Vin's request, I would be invited to the studio to watch the show. Working for Vin that summer was a wonderful experience. I must honestly say that Vin Di Bona is one of the classiest men I've ever met. He is kind, caring, and most of all a man of true generosity. I am honored to know him and most of all to call him my friend.

I got to hook up again with Joe Rocco. This time he contacted me to see if I were available and would be willing to do some TV spots for the New England Safety Dept. I said "yes", and we set up a meeting. In that meeting, Joe explained that I would play a character who would be taking on many different projects and do everything wrong regarding safety. The character's name was "Unsteady Eddie." While "Unsteady Eddie" would be endangering himself, he would be confronted by a safety specialist who would help "Unsteady Eddie" learn the necessary safety procedures. The safety guy was John La Conche who was an actual safety commissioner in the state of Connecticut. We did over 2 dozen of these spots which aired on TV in the New England area. The show was hosted by Joe Rocco who has since opened his own production company called RocJo Productions. Up until I moved to Los Angeles, Joe and I worked on the "Unsteady Eddie" project as well as many live stand up venues. Although I rarely get back to Rhode Island I will always remember all the standup gigs, the TV shows, and the friendly relationships I had with all the people I've worked with while I was still a Rhode Islander. It's something I'll never forget.

Chapter 29

While flying back to Rhode Island after a performance on a cruise ship in 1998 I just so happened to be seated next to a guy named Tony Bristol. He was the Program Director at WPRO a popular radio station in Rhode Island.

We made small talk and then he asked if I would like to host the station's 24th Anniversary at the Providence Performing Art Center. PPAC as it was better known, is an ornate movie theater complete with velvet seats spectacular chandeliers as well as elaborate artwork throughout. Tony listed the scheduled performers which included a boy band named *NSYNC. The Backstreet Boys were there also, but due to illness, the band did not perform that night. Headlining the show was Lisa Loeb with her backup Dweezil Zappa., the son of Frank Zappa. It was a packed house with over three thousand screaming fans. When I introduced *NSYNC, the crowd went wild. And the group did not disappoint. They blow the roof off the building. They were on fire and the crowd couldn't get enough. When they finished their act, I came back on stage to outro them and do a few jokes to settle the crowd down. It took me several minutes to finally restore some semblance of order. Now it was time to introduce Lisa. I gave her a great intro and I strongly encouraged the crowd to be respectful to the headliner. Now if you are familiar with *NSYNC and Lisa Loeb you would know that for a high energy act like *NSYNC followed by the mellow sounds of Lisa Loeb that could cause a problem. And boy oh boy did it! The crowd was unruly, to say the least. They were noisy and rude during Lisa's performance and her show crashed and burned. The radio station should have known better by having her go on after *NSYNC. It should have been the other way around. I felt bad for Lisa who was put into a no-win situation. After the show we were all in the green room and I had my family come back to meet and greet, and everyone was very affable. Lionel Ritchie was super, Lisa, who I could tell was feeling down, was still extremely cordial, and the entire group of *NSYNC were super friendly and respectful. At one point, Justin Timberlake signed my daughter Shawna's program writing "To Shawna, the prettiest girl in Rhode Island." Shawna was 15 at the time and was walking on air for several days after the concert. All in all, it was a great night in a classic venue which afforded me the opportunity to work with a group of amazing people.

As I mentioned, I moved to Los Angeles in 2000. I had just finished an engagement on a cruise ship and was headed to Los Angeles on a flight from Miami to set up my family. We had rented a furnished apartment in Studio City and while living there we would shop for a more permanent residence, either a house or a condo. As I boarded the plane in Miami, I recognized an incredibly famous couple sitting in first class. The husband was a famous comedian, writer, producer, and actor who made some of the most popular comedy movies of our generation. The wife was an actress who starred in many prominent films. I happened to have some comedy videos with me so I thought it would be a great opportunity if I could offer one of my DVD's to this comedy legend.

I asked the male flight attendant if I could go up to first class and offer them my DVD. The flight attendant said, "Let me take it to them". I anxiously awaited as he went up the aisle into first class. After several minutes, the attendant came through the curtains with a shocked look on his face. He approached my seat, handed me my DVD, and said, and I quote, "He cut me a new A-Hole" Now I am thinking, welcome to Hollywood. It certainly wasn't the welcome I was expecting.

Ironically, several years had passed and I was having dinner at Café Roma in Beverly Hills and who comes in and is seated at the table next to me. The very same comedian who refused my DVD on that flight to LA. I thought for a moment to speak to him and see if he recalled that incident. But on second thought, I figured it would be best to leave him alone. What could have been a cordial relationship never had the chance because of someone who just wasn't nice. Maybe he was having a bad day, received some bad news, who knows? However, I was taught early on in my career to always be great and recalling that day on the plane only reinforced it for me. Oh, I held back mentioning his name, but I will tell you it rhymes with "Bell Crooks."

In 2010 I got a call from the television show, Jimmy Kimmel Live. They wanted to do a sketch with me playing politician, Carl Palladino because I sort of looked like him. At that time, Palladino was making outrageous remarks and even threatening statements.

He once threatened a news reporter for allegedly taking pictures of his 10-year-old daughter. Palladino said, "I'll take you out, buddy." So, Kimmel writers thought it would be funny to have a sketch where Palladino is interviewed from the neck up and talking like a total badass. I was taken into the wardrobe and outfitted in a white tank top (wife beater) and daisy duke shorts. It was a very funny idea. The reporter would ask me questions and I, as Carl Palladino, would answer in a crude and coarse manner. This went on for a couple of minutes and when the interview concluded, the camera would peel back, revealing what I was wearing, and I would change my demeanor to a more effeminate posture.

Jimmy loved the sketch and when it aired, the audience roared with laughter. It was a fun shoot and I've been called back for other sketches, however as luck would have it, I missed a few due to sailing the high seas.

In 2013, while I was nursing Debra, I got a call from Christina Ferra-Gilmore, a Hollywood casting director who was a child actress most noted for her appearances on the Brady Bunch. I had the pleasure of working with her on other projects. She knew my situation and asked If I was up to audition for a role as a mob boss in a feature film. She promised she would have me wrapped in two hours. I asked Debra about it and she gave me her blessing. I asked Debra's dear friend Shirley if she would watch Debra for a few hours while I was shooting, and she said "of course". I knew Debra would be in the best of hands, so I decided to accept with the caveat that I would be checking in with Shirley frequently. The movie was a made-for-television film and it starred an actress by the name of Linda Blair. That's right, the same Linda Blair who starred in the original film "The Exorcist." What an unbelievable experience. Here I am doing a scene with Linda Blair who I remember vividly had scared the living daylights out of me. I spoke with her and told her that of all the movies I have watched in my life, not one film had such an impact on me as "The Exorcist" did. I told her I remembered slumping in my seat in the movie theater with chills all over my body. She was gracious and extremely friendly. I just had to tell her what the movie did to me. We chatted and she told me she is now working on rescuing dogs and has a farm with dozens of canines. It was a great pleasure to work with her and to get to know her at least for a short time. The movie was called *WHOA*, which stood for "Westfield Home Owners Association." In 2015, life was going well. Kristina and I were happy and the more time we were together, the more deeply in love we became. As of this writing, I can honestly say that my wonderful wife and I are becoming so close to each other that it feels like we've been together forever. My standup career was humming along with performances on luxury cruise liners, corporate events, and personal concerts. My acting career continued to flourish as well! I'm getting calls regularly from young casting directors to appear in their films. One day in 2016, I got a call from a young producer/director who owns Gear Mark Productions, and he asked me if I would be a part of his YouTube production called "Get-A-Waze." It was a spoof on the Waze app and in this production, I would play a mob boss (typecasting?) who uses the app to call a getaway car after robbing a home. It was a fun shoot. The producer liked me so much that he also booked me for another one of his projects. They are available on YouTube. With my acting going so well while still performing over 100 shows a year, to say my plate was full would be an understatement. 2017 started right where 2016 ended. I had secured multiple bookings for the year doing my standup, and my acting career was still on track with many projects in the works. One of the first things I did in 2017 was to book the role of a detective on a new Netflix TV show called "Deep Undercover." It was created and produced by Joe Pistone, who was the undercover FBI agent who took down the mafia. Hollywood released the movie "Donnie Brasco" based on Joe's undercover character. I became a regular on the show playing mostly mob bosses and detectives. The show was based on actual crimes and undercover sting operations. It was great fun and I loved the experience. Also, in 2017, I starred in a film called "The Hit." In it, I was a mob boss (getting the idea) who gets double-crossed by one of his minions. It was the first time I was killed on film, but it probably won't be the last. Also, that year, 2017, I auditioned for a film called "Czech Mate on Ice" It's a film about an immigrant family from Russia who come to the United States for a better life. With them is their young son whose dream is to be an NHL hockey player. The young man gets a job parking cars at the parking lot my character owns and operates. He and I begin to build a relationship and I become his mentor. I manage to persuade the local college hockey coach to give him a tryout. He passes with flying colors and later in the film he gets drafted by an NHL team.

The film was showcased at several film festivals and won an award for the best ensemble cast. The film is available on Amazon Prime. It was a great thrill to be a part of that amazing project.

Chapter 30

2018 was also a great year. I got booked for three feature films. The first one was a movie called "Unlawful Justice "also available on Amazon Prime. In it, I play a mean and nasty landlord who has no reservations about evicting his tenants who can't pay their rent. When I auditioned for the film, I was brought in to read for a detective role. But after the audition, the director liked my angry persona so much that he asked me to read for the landlord, which I did and booked the role on the spot. It was a great experience working with a very professional cast and crew. Also, in 2018, my standup was still going strong with more bookings coming than I could handle. The second film was a film called "This Much" which later was renamed "Bride to Be." What a great time I had filming this and being a part of an awesome cast and crew. In the film, I play the role of the neighbor who lives next door to a man and his Russian mail-order bride. Things don't go so well as the bride falls in love with their gardener and as their neighbor I get to see this unfold. The third film was a film done by a young man who worked at Sony Studios and was testing his wings for his very first solo project. It is a film about a young man that is trying to make a film but is having all sorts of problems as he is tormented by his doppelganger. It is called "Directorial." I portray director Martin Scorsese, who magically shows up to advise the young filmmaker. It was cool, and an honor to portray one of the greatest directors in film history. Finally, and what I thought was the coolest thing of all, I got an audition for a national product that was launching a new ad campaign. It turned out to be the newest ad for the product "Jimmie Choo's" shoes. I was called in to audition for a pizza shop owner, the audition went well and later I got a call saying I had booked the job. The producers decided to scrap the pizza shop owner's character and instead I was booked as a street hot dog vendor. It turns out the spokesperson for this campaign was Cara Delevingne, one of the world's top models and a fine young actress. My role was to serve her favorite hotdog as she was walking from one club to another in NYC. It was an awesome shoot and a great bunch of people to work with. The spot is on YouTube called "Shimmer in the Dark" and currently has 6.8 MILLION views. Once again in 2018, I got a call from an assistant casting director who asked me if I could be on set in an hour in wardrobe as a mob boss. I asked what it was, and he said a very high-profile music video. I said, "I'm on my way." Traffic was heavy and I stayed in constant phone communication with the AD. After an hour and a half of battling traffic I finally arrived. I was immediately rushed to the set where I met the star of the video. It happened to be Kendrick Lamar who has been regarded as one of the best and most influential artists of his generation. I got to hang out with him during the lulls in the shoot and he was very cool. It was an absolute thrill and honor to be featured in this video. The video also starred Rhianna; Unfortunately, she missed her flight that morning and they would shoot her stuff the next day. At last count, the video titled "Loyalty" had amassed over 191 MILLION views on YouTube.

Throughout my career, I've estimated that I have performed live to over one MILLON people, not including my film and television appearances. Although each laugh meant so much to me, there are two laughs that stand out in my career. The first one occurred at a six-star resort in Dixville Notch, New Hampshire. I was headlining at the Balsams Resort where the first votes are cast in the Presidential election. My show was in the "Edelweiss Room" a four hundred seat theater. It was a Saturday night and the room was filled. I began my show and it was going extremely well.

The crowd was awesome, and the laughs were coming in waves. Suddenly something unexpected happened. It was approximately ten minutes into my act when two couples walked in and made their way to the front of the room where staff members were setting up a table and four chairs for them. To say this action brought my show to a screeching halt would be an understatement. I knew I had to do something to relieve the tension, so I asked, "where were you guys?" and one of the men said, "we were moose hunting." Now you've heard about never heckling a comedian and in this case, it was as true as ever. I immediately shot back quote "it looks like you bagged a couple." The crowd exploded and it took about five minutes for them to settle down. The old saying "nobody likes a wise guy" rang true and the crowd let him know it. The other biggest laugh I got in my career took place while working on a cruise ship. I was cruising with Debra on a Royal Caribbean ship that had stopped at their private Island Coco Cay in the Bahamas for the day. The ship anchored and the passengers took tender boats to get to the island. As we were about to have lunch on the island, a staff member with a bullhorn was walking around announcing that a storm was coming, and everyone should head to the tender boats immediately after lunch. The storm came quicker than predicted and although some passengers were able to return to the ship, the waves got too high for the tenders to get the rest of the people back to the ship safely. Whoever didn't make it to the tender boats were forced to spend the night on the island. Debra and I had been at the beach, which was some distance from the ship. By the time we got the word it was too late, and we were left behind. We had no choice but to spend the night on Coco Cay. Well, as night fell the temperature started dropping and the people that were left on the island began erecting makeshift shelters. The cruise line did everything they could to help by using the man overboard speedboat to bring us supplies such as sweatshirts, T-shirts, and blankets. I found out later that the entire gift shop was emptied to bring us warm clothing. I must admit the passengers banded together to try to make the best of the situation. As the night wore on, and the temperature got colder, Debra and I decided to try to get some sleep. We secured a couple of lounge chairs, got some extra blankets, bundled up and eventually fell asleep. The next morning the crew staff brought over breakfast and around noon we all were cleared to tender back to the ship. As it turned out, I was working that night, and here's where the biggest laugh came in. I opened by welcoming everyone to the show, then I introduced my wife and explained that we didn't make it back to the ship. I went on stating that she had been with me on Coco Cay several times previously, and would always comment on how amazing it would be to spend a night on the island, so, in a booming voice I yelled quote, "Are you happy now?" The showroom erupted and the laughs lasted several minutes. Many times, after that incident, Debra and I would tell that story at parties or with friends and it would always generate explosive laughter.

In 1998, while I was still living in Rhode Island, my manager Dee from New York, called me with a corporate gig at the Yamashiro Restaurant located in the Hollywood Hills. It's a great restaurant with spectacular views of Hollywood and Los Angeles. The show was for a Dot.Com company. I accepted the gig and headed to Tinsel Town. I was picked up at LAX (Los Angeles International Airport) and driven to my hotel in downtown Los Angeles. My driver told me she would pick me up at 7:00 pm and take me to the location. We arrived at the venue at approximately 7:30. I was introduced to the two gentlemen who were the owners of the company; they were excited for me to be there and offered me dinner. The show was set for 9:00 pm. After dinner at approximately 8:45 pm, the owners told me they wanted to give out awards to their workers, and then I would go on. The banquet room was packed, and they seemed ready. Now, folks, I've done many corporate events leading up to this one, and from my experience, it is not good to do the awards first because most people have had dinner, received their award, and are ready to head home. I pled my case to go on before the awards, but to no avail. The owners insisted on doing the awards first. Now, keep in mind that LA people have a habit of leaving events early, baseball games, concerts, etc. So, it would be no surprise to me to see people leaving after the award ceremonies and leave they did in droves. By the time the last award was given out and I was introduced there were approximately 6 or 8 people left in the room. The owners sat right in the front, literally a few feet away from me. Let me insert here that the contract included paid airfare, paid hotel, paid expenses, and a fairly hefty check. So, a few minutes into my act, I could hear one owner say to the other, quote "we could have saved a lot money." Aside from the fee I received, I felt it was a waste of my time flying cross country to perform in front of a half dozen people. All because they wouldn't listen to someone who knew their craft. They deprived their workers of seeing a great comedy show. I hope in the future, these two dot. com guys realize it wasn't my fault but theirs by thinking they knew best. I can only hope that if they ever have another event they will heed the advice of a professional.

Sometimes the best-laid plans can run amuck. I was booked by Barry Katz to do a show in New Hampshire a few miles outside the Massachusetts state line. I was headlining the show and the feature act was a hot young comic named Denis Leary. I met Barry early for dinner, and as I got ready to leave my car wouldn't start. We tried to jump-start it, but it still wouldn't start. So, Barry said, "I have a comic's car you can use to get to the gig, and I'll call and get your car towed to a repair shop." The car that I was going to use was an older 80's Buick Sedan. Barry warned me that the gas gauge didn't work but he assured me I had enough gas to make it to the gig. Boy was he wrong. As I took the ramp to get on Route 93 heading towards New Hampshire I suddenly ran out of gas. Things went from bad to worse. As I was pushing the car off to the side of the road, the right front wheel went into a construction ditch. I tried pushing the car out of the ditch but to no avail. Approximately 15 to 20 minutes later I was able to flag down a group of young guys. They agreed to push me out of the ditch and bring me back a can of gasoline. Not too long after, they returned with a plastic jug of gasoline. I put the gas in, and luckily I got the car running and we were able to push it out of the ditch. I thanked the guys and I was off. However, I'm wasn't out of the woods yet. I still had to get to the gig, and I knew I had to stop for gas. After gassing up, I rushed to the gig as fast as I could hoping Leary would still on stage. I finally wheeled into the parking lot and I noticed Denis standing there with a small group of audience members as the rest of the crowd was filing out. I leaped out of the car and said, "I'm here." Leary said he did all he could to hold the crowd with a little over an hour of material. I asked the crowd, "Do you still want to do the show?" and everyone yelled 'yes". I thanked Denis for stretching his act and saving my butt. We all went back into the club and the crowd was awesome. It was a great show, and everyone said they were glad I finally made it.

Chapter 31

As a standup comedian, you are constantly at the risk of a calamity, and not many gigs have a bigger potential to be a disaster than a bachelor party. I recall one I did with a Boston comedy legend named Bob Seibel. Bob was a funny guy on and off the stage. I remember arriving early as usual at a hall somewhere outside the Boston area. I surveyed the situation; I rather quickly knew this was going to be a "Hell Gig." Bob arrived a little bit later and asked me how it looked. I told him not good. Bob was slated to go on first and I would close the show. When it came time to start the show, the crowd was already drunk and rowdy, to say the least. The groom's brother introduced Bob and from the very beginning, he was being heckled unmercifully. Not just your run-of-the-mill heckles, but vile, disgusting obscenities and references. Shockingly, midway through Bob's set the groom jumped on stage and took out his penis and started dancing around Bob.

Seibel, being the pro that he was, did his best to restrain himself while trying to laugh off the situation. Luckily, the groom's brother came up and convinced him to get off the stage. Bob managed to finish his set, get off the stage, get paid, and leave as quickly as possible. The groom's brother introduced me, and at this point it was total chaos.

Luckily, I didn't have to deal with the groom's penis. I plowed through my act amid the heckles, boos, and a constant chant of "You Suck." When it was mercifully over, the groom came over to me and paid me in cash. As I was gathering myself together, the groom's brother came over to me and said thanks and handed me some cash. Now, normally, I would have told him that his brother had already paid me, but because of the abuse I took for 45 minutes I felt I deserved the extra money. A couple of weeks later I was booked with Seibel on another gig and we talked about that night at the bachelor party. When I told Bob that I got paid twice, he responded with his usual response, which he was known for. He said, "You hot shit" and we laughed together for a while.

I guess I have been a "comedian" and an actor as far back as I can remember even though I didn't know it at the time. I would always do (I guess you could call them) primitive sketches. I would also make my friends laugh by saying silly things along with some outrageous antics. Here are several examples of the stunts I did as a young boy and goofy things I would say, especially in elementary school. Why did I do them? Because I just loved making people laugh. As a young teenager, I would do all sorts of silly stuff to make my friends laugh. Once I came up with this idea of filling my mouth with candy to make it appear that my cheeks were swollen. Back in the day you could buy penny candy, which was an individual piece of candy for one penny. I bought 5 Mary Jane's which was a kind of taffy with nuts in it. So, the sketch was, I would be riding my bike and pretend to fall and wait for a Good Samaritan to help me. When that person would come to help me, I would turn my face to show my swollen cheek. The Good Samaritan would freak out and want to take me to the hospital, that's when I would show him, I had a mouthful of candy. My friends would be on the sidelines laughing their heads off. Another time, while playing outside (yes you could do that back then) my friend and I found an old crutch in someone's trash can, so I came up with this sketch. I would be standing at an intersection on the crutch and as soon as there were car traffic my friend would come up to me, push me down and start hitting me with the crutch. Once a "Good Samaritan" would come out of his car to my rescue, my friend and I would take off running leaving the "Good Samaritan" standing there wondering what just happened. Once far enough away, my friend and I would laugh until our stomachs ached. I guess the comedy was in my DNA from the moment I was born. It just got muddled because of my fear and doubt and lacking the courage to abandon everything I knew and just go for it. One time in school, the teacher asked us to write down certain jobs in our local department store, why our teacher asked us that question remains a mystery to this day. Anyway, sitting in class next to me was a new kid who just moved to Rhode

Island from Ohio. He always thought I was hysterical, maybe because of the east coast attitude he had never experienced while living in Ohio, or maybe because I was just flat out funny. Anyway, as we were writing down various jobs found in a department store, we would check out each other's paper. One of the jobs I wrote down was "scrub woman." It was a term I had heard before and I thought it meant some kind of cleaning lady. When David, from Ohio, glanced over and saw my paper with "scrub woman" on it, he lost it, which made me feel good because I made him laugh. He was laughing so hard that I started to crack up, which drew the attention of our teacher who wanted to know what we were howling about. Of course, we said nothing. He asked us to bring up our paper and when he didn't find anything offensive or vulgar, he just separated us from each other. It was situations like that which made me believe I could be a comedian, but again, I had no clue on how to do it. As I got older and more mature, I began to realize that my comedic talent must have come from my dad. As I mentioned earlier, he was in vaudeville, and according to him, he loved it. Could my dad have been a successful comedian? I believe so, but I also know that he didn't have the wherewithal to pursue it. He got married at a young age, had kids, and because of that, he didn't go after it. Unknowingly, I sort of followed in his footsteps. Luckily, I never gave up on my dream, even though at times it got lost. Sadly, my Dad didn't do the same.

Keep in mind, my dad passed away in 1984. Aside from the pain of losing a loved one, it was also heartbreaking to me that he never got to see me do standup. Would he have been proud of me? I believe he would have. My dad didn't talk much about his days in vaudeville, and if he did it was because my brother and I would drag it out of him. Did he not talk about it because he never followed up, or because it was a bittersweet memory? I'll never know. What I do know is if my dad had encouraged me to go after my dream, my career might have gone in an entirely different direction. My dad was old school Italian and having heart to heart talks was not on his radar. Also, my mom was an overprotective Italian mother and would not support me moving to New York or Los Angeles, at 16, to become a comedian, True to form, in the end my dad would not go against my mom's wishes. But unknowingly, something inside was telling me to attend that bachelor party. When I was told I could do an open mic at a comedy club, my heart surged. Without thinking of anything that was going on in my life, sheer instinct made me say "yes". True, I did start later in life, but maybe it had to go that way. Who knows, it's possible I could have gone to New York or Los Angeles and because I was so young and naïve, I could have failed, lost faith, become discouraged and depressed and head back to Rhode Island thinking I gave it a shot and it just wasn't meant to be. That's something else I'll never know. But one thing I do know, I have managed to clear all the hurdles that were in my path to get to where I am today, and for me now there is no looking back, just straight ahead, living my dream. Every day I am thankful that I'm able to do what I love and to bring joy and laughter into people's lives just for that one hour we spend together. Those are special moments in my life, moments I'll never forget.

Several times a year I would headline at a family resort adjacent to the Pocono Mountains called Woodloch Pines. In 1997 while still living in Rhode Island I would make the 4-hour drive from my house to eastern Pennsylvania. Generally, my wife Debra would come with me and one late fall engagement we had our teen age daughter Shawna with us. I had to board a cruise ship the very next day, so the plan was to rise early in the morning after the show, and drive directly to the airport in Providence, and the girls would drop me off and head home. That night after I finished my show, which was around 11:30 pm, we headed back to our room and noticed that snow flurries had started. Now, I've done the gig many times and it was a good 10-12-mile drive on a two-lane road with many hills to reach the highway. So, I knew if the snow continued it would be a difficult drive to get Route 84. I changed the plans and decided that instead of 6:00 am we would leave at 4:00 am giving us 8 hours to complete a 4-hour drive just in case the storm intensified. We fell asleep at around midnight and when we woke up at 4:00 am the ground was covered, and it was snowing heavily. We loaded up our car, a 1996 Saturn, and began our drive. I thought we would be okay because the Saturn had front-wheel drive. However, the snow kept mounting and, because it was so early, the snowplows hadn't come out yet. I knew this would be a tremendous challenge. I recall one hill in particular. I was having a terrible time trying to get up and over it, the tires were spinning, and I could hear the whizzing sound as the car's engine strained to make it to the top. I knew at that point if I didn't get up and over this hill, we were going to be stuck there for who knows how long. I was new with the cruising industry and heard if for any reason you miss the ship you would be fired. With the accelerator pedal pressed to the floor, the engine roaring, the tires spinning, and the Saturn swerving, we crept our way until we managed to get over this imposing obstacle. However, we were far from out of the woods. What started as a snow flurry around midnight turned into a full-blown white-out! I was only able to drive safely at approximately 15-20 miles an hour without sliding out of control. At approximately 7:00 am we managed to get to a small town because by now parts of the highway was closed. There was a diner there and we had a quick breakfast and then I called my agent Dee from a payphone (remember those) and told her the situation. She said, "I'll get on it". We jumped back in the car and started driving. About 30-45 minutes later we stopped at a gas station to call my agent back. She had a plan ready for us. She booked me on a flight out of Bradley Airport in Hartford, Connecticut to Miami where the ship was docked. The flight was to leave at some time after 1:00 pm and arrive in Miami around 4:00 pm. From the airport, I was to jump in a cab and head to the ship. Now all I had to do was get to Bradley. However, I was concerned for my wife and daughter and if they could get home safely. Debra assured me she would be careful and make it home safe. After a 9-hour tortuous, treacherous drive we arrived at Bradley airport. When we got there my heart sunk. The whole place was covered in deep snow. I'm thinking there is no way any planes are flying out of here. I pulled up to the door, grabbed my stuff, kissed Debra, and Shawna who, believe it or not, slept through most of the ordeal, and ran into the airport. Security was light, to say the least. Remember this was 1997. Debra had told me she'd wait until she would see my plane take off. I never dreamed it would, but the counter person gave me my boarding pass and told me to hurry to the gate. Amazingly, I boarded the plane and we took off. When I landed in Miami, I immediately called Debra to see if she made it home safely, which she did, and to let her know I had landed, and I was headed to the ship. I jumped in a cab and was on my way. By now, it was close to 5:30 pm and the ship was scheduled to sail away at 5:00 pm. So, I wasn't even sure if the ship would be there when I arrived. With a sigh of relief, it was still there. As I boarded the ship, I was greeted by the cruise director who instead of doling out pleasantries, said "I held the ship for you, so you better be funny." I knew it was said tongue in cheek because I found out later that they held the ship while waiting on some passengers who also encountered foul weather. So, next time you see a comedian and think what a great way to make a living, sometimes it has its moments.

Chapter 32

After Debra and I moved to Los Angeles, we would go back to Chicago several times a year to visit family and friends. While there, I would also perform at various Zanies Comedy Clubs. On one Chicago visit, we heard about an Italian restaurant in Bloomingdale, Illinois called Spavone's. Debra and I decided to try it along with some friends. We loved it. The food was delicious, and we had a wonderful evening. During dinner, Tony, the owner, would walk among the tables singing Italian songs.

We became regulars whenever we got back to Chicago. On one occasion as we were leaving I approached Tony and started a conversation. I asked if he performs at other venues and he mentioned he does a lot of the Italian festivals I told him I was a standup comic, living in Los Angeles and that when I visit Chicago, I perform at Zanies. He surprised me when he said, "Maybe we could do a comedy show here next time you're in town." I said, "that sounds great". Tony and I would talk on the phone about doing the show and then we decided to move forward. In July 2004, I went ahead and booked a Fri-Sat-Sun at Zanies. The show at Tony's would be the following Thursday. Debra and I would stay with our best friends in Chicago, Ed, and Sheila Ahern. The weekend at Zanies went great, now we could just hang out until Thursday. The night of the show we arrived at Spavone's and it was jam-packed. The crowd loved the show and gave me a standing ovation. What I found out that night, the reason Tony scheduled the show on Thursday, was that he was performing that weekend at the Italian Festival in Milwaukee. Tony invited Debra and me, along with Ed and Sheila, to attend the show as his guests. We gladly accepted. At the festival, there are five different stages throughout the grounds. We went to Tony's show at 5:00 pm and it went great.

The crowd loved him. I will tell you; Tony Spavone is an exceptionally talented Italian tenor. After his show, we went backstage to congratulate him and also to thank him for inviting us. He was gracious and thanked us for coming. We noticed his wife and children were also in the room and we wanted to give them some personal time, so once again we thanked him and left.

There were two shows scheduled for later that evening starting at 9 p.m. One show was starring Frankie Avalon, the other show was starring Nancy Sinatra. We grabbed some greasy but delicious Festival Food and decided to check out Frankie Avalon's show. When we got there, it was overflowing with people trying to find a vantage point. There was not a seat to be found. So, we then headed to the Nancy Sinatra show. When we arrived, after a short walk, we noticed it was very crowded. However, there were some seats left. We managed to get four seats together quite a distance from the stage. After a short wait, Nancy came out and opened her show with a Cher tune, written by Sonny Bono, titled "Bang Bang You Shot Me Down", which Nancy also recorded in 1966. The song went over okay but what happened next was astounding. Her second number was a heavy metal tune which I have never heard of. Midway through that song, the crowd started leaving like there was a bomb scare. We remained for her next number and it was more of the same, so we also left. I had later mentioned this to Tony, and he confided in me that the entertainment director had told him it was the worst financial disaster in his entertainment career. Tony and I had become good friends and did more shows at his restaurant. On one particular visit Tony told me that he was putting together a show at Navy Pier in Chicago with himself, Joey Dee and The Starliters, known for their hit record "The Peppermint Twist". Tony asked if I would like to perform on the show. I said "of course". The show was scheduled for later in the year. I booked some comedy club gigs in the Chicago area sandwiched around the Navy Pier date. The day of the show the bleachers were filled to capacity. I did double duty on the show as a host/comic. I opened the show with a few announcements and then went into my act. I rattled off a snappy 30-minute set that went fantastic. I finished and after the applause, I introduced Joey Dee and The Starliters, consisting of Joey Dee, Dave Brugatti, of The Young Rascals fame, and Bobby Valli, Frankie Valli's brother. They were great guys and their show was tremendous. I went back on stage and introduced Tony, who had a large contingent of friends and family in the audience. Tony's show went extremely well ending in a standing ovation. All in all, it was an exciting fun day working with Tony and Joey Dee and The Starliters. I still talk to Tony, but due to my acting career, I don't get to travel as much as I used to.

I met Jamie Farr in February 2002 at a celebration for my best friend Fred Travalena who was receiving his star on the Hollywood Walk of Fame. Jamie and I talked for a few minutes about his golf tournament and the show M.A.S.H. I mentioned I was a standup comedian and we chatted about comedy and then I told him my opening joke in my act was, "Folks I know you're looking at me thinking, you know if Tony Bennett and Klinger from M.A.S.H could ever have a child it would look like me."

I did not get a laugh from him, instead, he said, "Change it to Jamie Farr." With all due respect, I think most people would recognize him as the character Klinger as opposed to Jamie Farr. And ironically enough in our photo, I don't believe we look alike at all. Perhaps more so in our younger days. However, to this day I still open with that joke and it continues to get a big laugh. No disrespect Mr. Farr, but when I do the joke, I say Tony Bennett and Klinger from M.A.S.H. I have found by being in this business for a long time most actors do not like being identified as their character. I think it is a great honor to be looked upon as a particular character.

While I was in the process of writing this book something amazing happened. I had gotten off a cruise ship and was sitting in the Juneau Alaska airport waiting for my flight home when I get an email from Victoria Thomas's office. She is a major casting director in Hollywood, casting such films as "Django Unchained," "The Great Wall," "Fences," "Straight Outta Compton, "42-The Jackie Robinson Story" just to name a few, so I knew this was a big deal. The email asked me if I was available for the following days, July 30, 31, and August 1st and 2nd, 2018. Unfortunately, I was only available for July 30th and 31st, so I emailed that information back to her office, knowing that in most cases if you are not available for all the dates mentioned they move on. At that point I felt dejected. However approximately a half-hour later her office emails me back asking if I'm available on July 26th. I immediately emailed back that I was available.

I got an email back booking me for a movie, and I would be sent all the pertinent information. As it turned out I was right, it was a big deal. It was supposedly for a role in a movie called "Magnum Opus" which I later found out was a fake name. I did some snooping around and learned that the actual film was titled "Once Upon A Time in Hollywood". It was a new film directed by Quentin Tarrantino and starring Leonardo DiCaprio, Brad Pitt, Al Pacino, and Margo Robbie. Several days after returning home I was asked to come into wardrobe for a fitting. I was fitted with suits of various styles and colors. Some were single breasted, and some were double breasted, that's when the costume designer let the cat out of the bag. One time when she was shown a double-breasted suit she said, "We can't have him in a double breasted, Al is wearing one" I knew right then I must be in a scene with Al Pacino. The costume designer decided she wanted me in a black suit, but they didn't have one in the wardrobe department to fit me. The wardrobe crew apologized and asked if I could come back the next day. Of course, I agreed. When I returned for a fitting the next day the wardrobe crew was ready. They had purchased an elegant three-piece black suit. The costume designer loved it and said, "go with it". When I first arrived in Hollywood in 2000 one of my goals was to be in a film with either one or both of my heroes, Robert De Niro and Al Pacino. I can now check off the Al Pacino box. When all this was happening, Kristina was incredibly happy for me. The day of the shoot rolled around, and I was to meet at base camp, a holding area for craft services and other actors who had smaller roles. I was then taken by van service to the set which was the interior of a large ornate downtown LA restaurant with a 50's-60's vibe. All cellphones were confiscated so no pictures could be taken. I got into wardrobe and waited on the set. After a short while, Al Pacino showed up. Just like I did with Tom Hanks I suddenly became star struck. I couldn't believe it. Me, standing next to Al Pacino. Then, director Quentin Tarrantino came onto the set wearing a pair of black and white sneakers with Kill Bill in red letters on them. Al and Quentin didn't say much but wanted to run the scene which meant doing the scene without the cameras on. As we were getting ready, Leonardo DiCaprio walks onto the set to say hi to Al Pacino which placed him about six inches from me. He said hi to me hugged Al and said to Al "if you need anything, I'll be upstairs" and with that he walked off. I froze for a moment in time. Incredibly, I was inches away from Leonardo DiCaprio and Al Pacino and just several feet away from Quentin Tarrantino. Is this a dream or is this my dream coming to fruition? My scene with Al Pacino would be him sitting at a table in my restaurant on the phone when I walk in. Al tells whoever is on the other line to hold on. He then orders a drink from me. I tell him "yes, Mr. Schwarz" (not Schwartz) Tarrantino made this clear, later in the scene. I bring Al his drink he thanks me, and I say, "certainly sir", and I walk off. It was a mind-boggling experience. We did a bunch of takes as Quentin kept tweaking Al's lines. Finally, after another take, Tarrantino yelled cut and print. We were done. As Al got up from his seat, I said, "I love your amazing work and it's a phenomenal thrill to meet you and a dream come true to work with you". Al Pacino thanked me for the kind words and walked away to get ready for his next scene. A few moments later I was driven back to base camp, changed clothes, did some paperwork, thanked everyone, and left. They did have a ride for me back to the parking lot, but it was only three blocks, so I decided to walk. I wanted to walk to have a moment to myself to soak it all in. On my way to the parking garage, I noticed the crew was setting up for the next shot of Al Pacino in a pristine vintage Rolls- Royce. As I turned the corner, I saw Quentin Tarrantino sitting in a director's chair just waiting for the next shot. I took the liberty to approach him and thank him for the opportunity and he said, "You did a great job." He went on to say, "you pronounced Schwarz even better than Al did". What a great compliment and what an amazing experience, and as I look back, I sometimes wonder when I'm going to wake up from this dream.

Chapter 33

My mom was an exceedingly difficult person in many ways. She didn't trust anybody, including friends, relatives, and various people she would meet. Because of that I never got close to any of my cousins, uncles, aunts, or even grandparents. I wasn't allowed to bring my friends into our house and my mom would constantly tell my siblings and me to watch out for other people. She never liked anyone who met her children, even when we got into relationships. She never gave any one of us her blessing, quite the contrary. She would start trouble by accusing our boyfriends, girlfriends, and later our spouses, of committing various injustices. She was a very tough woman, capable of ripping a telephone book in half, which I witnessed several times. One time, my brother "Duke" had gotten into a fight with another kid and a bunch of friends of the other kid joined in seriously outnumbering my brother. I recall 'Duke" running toward our house yelling for help. My mom was the only one home beside me, so she grabbed a baseball bat and chased them all away. My mom didn't have much formal education, but she was blessed with an abundance of common sense. As tough as she was, with her children she was as gentle as a lamb. She loved her kids tremendously and displayed great love and affection for all of us. When one of us would get a cut or scrape, my mom was there with loving care.

I recall, when I was young, asking her if she was a nurse. My mother was also an exceedingly difficult person to understand. She had so many issues, which made it hard to deal with her. I'm sure by today's standards my mom would have needed counseling, but it was a different world back then. All my siblings just thought that's how mom was.

In the end, I'm left with so many memories of my mom. Some are wonderful and some are horrendous, but through it all, I loved her and respected her to the utmost. Growing up in all Italian culture, I was told many times by friends and other Italians that you only have one mother.

My dad was a very smart person when it came to knowing a lot about sports, history, and general knowledge. However, unlike my mom, he lacked common sense. I believe he never got a handle on how to be a dad either. He was extremely strict and rigid in his thoughts and displayed a great deal of stubbornness. It was impossible to reason with him. My feeling is that he was overwhelmed by having six children and was incapable of handling it. I never had a man to man talk with my dad, ever. I don't recall him ever kissing me or telling me he loved me. Honestly, my dad was not a warm person who could sit and explain things about growing up and life in general. It was his way or the highway, which he stated many times. My dad was also extremely jealous of my mom, which led to numerous verbal conflicts between them. I believe that my dad absolutely loved my mom with all his heart but lacked the skills to assure a happy marriage. My years living with my parents were filled with turbulence. But here's the kicker to all of this: when my mom passed away, I was filled with sorrow and mourned her loss. But when my dad passed away, I shocked myself because at his funeral I broke down badly. I was sobbing so much I had to be consoled by friends and family. I found it ironic that I acted that way. It only proves how important it is for a child to have a father figure in their life. Although my father was strict, stern, and void of affection, he was always there. I felt good knowing that I had a dad.

My dad never had a drink of alcohol in his entire life so that certainly was not the cause of his anger and mostly his frustration. In the end, I just believe he was overwhelmed and perhaps he felt he made a mistake and regretted what he did with his life.

Before I continue I want to make it clear, not all auditions go as smoothly as some that I had previously mentioned. In fact, going out on auditions, whether for acting or comedy can be a very frustrating ordeal. The average Hollywood actor would book a role in approximately 1 out of 17 auditions. Luckily for me, my average is somewhat less than that. That doesn't mean it's all peaches and cream. In my career, I have felt so many emotions. As an actor I had to learn to accept rejection, disappointment, insecurities, and even exasperation. I've had so many callbacks that I thought I nailed, but for whatever reason, the role went to another actor. One I vividly remember was a Budweiser national commercial. The theme was Joe Buck's (Sportscaster for Fox Sports) agent was telling Joe the reason he wasn't more successful was that he didn't have a famous catchphrase. So, I got a call from my agent, Stuart, that he got me an audition for this Budweiser spot as a typical New York agent.

. I was thrilled because this was in my wheelhouse. The audition went great as I did catchphrases from other great broadcasters. Lines like Phil Rizzuto's "Holy Cow", Mel Allen's "How about that", Chris Berman's "He could go all the way", and Dave Johnson's race call "And down the stretch they come." I did the entire audition as a dyed in the wool New Yorker. It went so well that I got a call back. The callback went great as well. Then Stuart called me and said the sponsors and director wanted a second callback. On the second callback, I crushed it and I felt strongly that I would be booked. Unfortunately for me, the role went to another actor. Now here's the part I have trouble understanding, I saw the commercial on TV and it was a complete flop. (no sour grapes) I think it aired only once or twice. The actor they chose didn't look or act like a New Yorker at all. He reminded me of an insurance salesman from the Midwest. I was disappointed, but in my business, you have to learn not to take it personally. There could have been several reasons why they went with someone else. The real job of an actor is to give the best audition you can and when you leave knowing you did, put it out of your mind. If you book the project, that's the cherry on top of the cake.

The following is a list, in no particular order, of the many celebrities I've worked with over the course of my career.

1. Linda Blair
2. Roy Orbison
3. Connie Francis
4. Henny Youngman
5. Robert Goulet
6. Frankie Valli
7. Angela Bassett
8. Angie Dickinson
9. Tiny Tim
10. Natalie Cole
11. Jackie Mason
12. Gallagher

13. Regis Philbin
14. Jay Leno
15. Smokey Robinson
16. Dan Ackroyd
17. Rodney Dangerfield
18. Jamie Foxx
19. Tom Hanks
20. Charo
21. Sherman Hemsley
22. Lionel Ritchie
23. Fred Travalena
24. Jimmy Kimmel
25. Neil Sedaka
26. Bowzer
27. Bob Eubanks
28. Taylor Dayne
29. George Takei
30. Ann Jefferies
31. Jaime Farr
32. Tommy Lasorda
33. Herb Reed (original member of the Platters)
34. B.J. Thomas
35. The Crystals
36. David Paymer
37. Rich Jeni
38. The Box tops
39. Dave Coulier
40. Tavares
41. Florence LaRue
42. Debbie Gibson
43. John Savage
44. 'NSYNC
45. Adam Ant
46. Chubby Checker
47. Andrew "Dice" Clay
48. John Byner
49. Dion
50. Paulie Shore
51. Melissa Leo
52. The Guess Who
53. The Drifters
54. Corey Hart
55. Lisa Loeb
56. Dweezil Zappa
57. Bobby Vinton
58. Ben Vereen
59. Conan O'Brien
60. The Doobie Brothers (Michael McDonald)
61. Jimmie Walker
62. Vinny Pazienza
63. Tab Hunter
64. Rita Moreno
65. Dennis Farina
66. Mike Nichols
67. Jim Nabors
68. Joey Dee
69. Dave Brugatti
70. Bobby Valli
71. Pamela Anderson
72. Kendrick Lamar
73. Pat Boone
74. Patrick Timsit
75. Lou Gossett Jr.
76. Marylyn McCoo
77. Kevin Nealon
78. Jay Cohen
79. The Beach Boys
80. Bill Burr
81. Al Pacino
82. Barbara Hershey

83. Ron Perlman	87. Al Martino
84. John Davidson	88. Billy Crystal
85. Marty Allen	89. Louis C.K.
86. Billy Davis Jr	

This list consists of celebs I have worked with, but not taken photos with.

1. Quentin Tarrantino
2. The Temptations
3. Huey Lewis + The News
4. Philip Seymour Hoffman
5. Julia Roberts
6. Jerry Seinfeld

And many more

Chapter 34

Being a comedian and actor has made my wildest dreams come true. Not only that but can you imagine how exciting it is for me to work with people who I admired as a child. People like John Byner who I loved when I was young and always was excited when he would appear on TV. Then to appear on a national TV comedy show (A&E's Comedy on the Road) hosted by him was so incredible. People like Dion of Dion and the Belmonts, a group I loved as a teenager and danced to their music and then to open for Dion was overwhelming.

What has happened to me in my career has been electrifying and I've relished every second of it.

As I close this saga of my life, I still will continue to do what I love. I'd like to take this page to thank all the comedians who inspired me as a child. Of course, they didn't know me but just watching them on TV made me want to be like them. I fell in love with their style, their ability to make people laugh, to come out on stage, and take command of the situation. I wanted so much to do what they were doing. Even as a young boy I would try extremely hard to feel what they were feeling. To me, the comedians of my generation were the epitome of cool. Even the way they dressed. Tuxedos, fancy suits, big chunky rings on their pinkies, all of it made me want it more and more. I've had second thoughts about my career, and now with all I've accomplished over the years, I honestly believe in my mind, had I gone to New York or Los Angeles when I was just a teenager, I might be a household name today. I would have started my career with people like Jay Leno, David Letterman, Rodney Dangerfield, Richard Pryor, George Carlin, Frank Gorshin, Rip Taylor, Alan King, Phyliss Diller, George Kirby, Charlie Callas, Guy Marks, Buddy Hackett, and Don Rickles. I'm sure I left some names out and I apologize for that. One thing for sure is I'll never really know. What I do know is I've had an amazing career up to this point and I will continue to make people laugh until it is no longer physically or mentally possible for me. I would like to thank the Rhode Island comics who gave me my start Frank O'Donnell and Charlie Hall. Special thanks to Barry Katz for literally launching my career.

Finally, I want to give unmatched thanks to my beautiful wife Kristina for her unwavering support, love, and understanding. I also want to thank her for continually inspiring me to be a better comedian and more importantly a better person. I'm so happy she has chosen to stand shoulder to shoulder with me as I continue to follow my dream. She is an incredibly special person and I'm so lucky to be married to such an amazing woman.

By the way, did I mention that I am living proof that a forgotten dream can become a reality.

The End

G. Hammerling
Trainer

POWER BIT
2nd Johnstown Flood
3rd Calabria

A. Winant
7 Furlongs
Time 1.29.1
April 5, 1963

G. Hammerling
Owner &
Trainer

EARL OF TYRONE
2nd Twin Spruce
3rd Triple Five

A. Winant Up
1 Mile
Time 1.42
April 5, 1963

G. Hammerling
Owner &
Trainer

PROVENDER SAM
2nd Mortal Combat
3rd Our Gain

D. Madden Up
5 Furlongs
Time 1.01
Feb. 27, 1963

Linda Blair

Ben Vereen

Rita Moreno

Frankie Valli

N'Sync

Jamie Foxx

Henny Youngman

Regis Philbin

Jimmie Walker

Charo

Rodney Dangerfield

Billy Crystal

Chubby Checker

Jamie Farr

Al Jardine

Bobby Vinton

Tom Hanks

Mike Nichols

Natalie Cole   Ron Perlman

Fred Travalena

Michael McDonald (The Doobie brothers)